# Japanese for Beginners

## 2 Books in 1
## Sushi Cookbook and Ramen Cookbook

### 200 Quick and Easy Recipes to Make a Perfect Dinner at Home

MAGGIE BARTON

# CONTENTS

# RAMEN COOKBOOK ...........................188

## EASY – 15/30 MINUTES ...............................189

# HARD – 90+ MINUTES

# Sushi Cookbook

## Quick and Easy Recipes to Make Healthy Sushi at Home

MAGGIE BARTON

# INTRODUCTION

The Japanese sushi dish has never been more popular than it is now. Previously it was often eaten as a side dish in other restaurants, but nowadays there are numerous specialized sushi restaurants. You can now also find sushi in supermarkets in all kinds of different shapes. Sushi is popular for a good reason, because it is not only tasty, but also healthy. The main ingredients of sushi, rice, fish and vegetables are all considered healthy as they contain many different vitamins. In addition, sushi is easy to digest and made from fresh products.

Thanks to the fresh vegetables used to make sushi, you get your much needed antioxidants and the fish provides your daily vitamins and minerals. Not only the sushi itself is healthy, the soy sauce also has health benefits. Soy is good for your bones and circulation and wasabi has an antibacterial effect. Sushi has many health benefits, but of course it depends on how you eat sushi. If you choose to make sushi yourself, make sure that the fish you use is safe to eat raw. For Healthy sushi, it is better to leave out the fat dips and use the soy sauce sparingly. In short, sushi can be a very healthy and tasty meal, but pay attention to how big your portion is and how many extras you put on your rice rolls.

# DIFFERENT TYPES OF SUSHI

## NIGIRI SUSHI

Nigiri Sushi consists of a small portion of sticky rice, which is shaped with the hands. Depending on the type of sushi, a piece of fish (salmon, tuna) or vegetables is placed on it. Depending on your taste, you can also combine it with wasabi paste.

## MAKI-SUSHI

In Maki-Sushi the rice is wrapped in dried seaweed (nori). For this you need a bamboo mat. Salmon, shrimp or tuna are best suited for the filling. You can also incorporate cucumber sticks, carrot sticks or spring onions.

## TEMAKI-SUSHI

In contrast to Nigiri-Sushi, Temaki-Sushi is more like a school bag. The rice is also packed in nori, but the algae leaf is rolled up conically. In addition, the typical sushi ingredients such as fish (shrimp, salmon) and vegetables are used again.

## CALIFORNIA ROLLS

California rolls are less common in Japan, but are very popular in Europe. The basic ingredients are similar to maki sushi, but are processed the other way round. The nori sheets are inside, the rice outside. Some sesame seeds or salmon roe decorate this sushi variant.

# 10 REASONS TO EAT SUSHI

## 1. SUSHI COMES IN A LOT OF VARIATIONS

There are a lot of different types of sushi. So there will always be a sushi that you appreciate. Moreover, eating sushi will not get bored that way. Every time you put a different variant on your plate.

## 2. SUSHI IS HEALTHY

Sushi is known as a healthy food. After all, it is prepared with various fresh fish, vegetables, so full of vitamins, and rice. If you are a fan of vegetarian food, there are still the countless veggie variants with only delicious vegetables. This means that even if you are a vegetarian, you can enjoy sushi.

## 3. SUSHI IS EASY TO DIGEST

The ingredients that sushi is made of make this an easily digestible meal. Because sushi is not heavy on your stomach, it is an excellent meal to eat at noon. So replace your lunch with sushi and make it something special, but also very tasty. Of course this also applies if you replace your dinner with different types of sushi, because even then the meal will be easy to digest and very tasty. Fortunately, after eating, sometimes even huge amounts of sushi, the annoying bloating does not occur. So you can always put sushi on the menu.

## 4. EATING SUSHI IS FUN

Eating sushi is an excellent way to enjoy yourself with your loved ones. After all, enjoying different delicious sushi variants together is very pleasant. Moreover, there will usually be laughed a lot. Eating sushi with chopsticks will undoubtedly create laughable situations that will certainly enhance the atmosphere at the table. Once you've eaten sushi, look forward to your next sushi date.

## 5. SUSHI IS ALWAYS FRESH FOOD

Because only fresh ingredients are used for the preparation of sushi, you can be sure that no nutrients will be lost. You are also sure that you do not receive products that have passed the expiry date. In most restaurants where sushi is on the menu, these delicious snacks are almost made in front of you. Because the preparation is very fast, you will never have to wait long before you can enjoy.

## 6. SUSHI IS A FEAST FOR THE EYES

When you eat, the eye wants something. For that reason, sushi is ideal to put on the table. The presentation of these delicious snacks is often done in a very beautiful and creative way. You can think of sushi that is brought to the table in the form of a boat. Almost a shame to eat, but also too tasty to leave.

## 7. YOU CAN ALSO PREPARE SUSHI AT HOME

While many great sushi restaurants exist, you can also choose to prepare these treats at home. The preparation of sushi is not really difficult because you hardly have to cook (only the rice). After preparing sushi, your kitchen doesn't have to look like a pigsty. You also don't have to toil for hours in the kitchen before you can finally get to the table.

## 8.  PREPARING SUSHI CANNOT GO WRONG

The preparation of sushi can hardly go wrong because you don't have to bake anything. Therefore, no products can burn, so your meal will end up in the trash. You do not have to be a kitchen prince or princess to serve a delicious sushi meal to your family and friends. In addition, there are special sushi kits on the market that contain everything you have left for preparing a sushi meal. Of course, such a kit also contains all the information you need to prepare the dishes.

## 9.  SUSHI IS ALSO DELIVERED AT HOME

When you don't feel like going to a sushi restaurant, but don't want to prepare these tasty snacks yourself, there are also companies that deliver the desired sushi at home. In recent years, these companies have sprung up all over the country like mushrooms. So there will probably be one in your area. You no longer even have to leave your home to eat tasty sushi, just order and pay by phone or via the internet, and the goodies will be delivered to any desired address within seconds.

## 10. SUSHI BOWL IS ALSO POSSIBLE

If you want to serve sushi to your guests in a special way, you can also choose to make a sushi bowl. For this you only have to put the desired ingredients in a bowl. So you don't have to roll sushi. This is perhaps the simplest way to enjoy sushi. You can make a sushi bowl almost anywhere, anytime.

# NUTRIENTS IN SUSHI

Many sushi lovers would not hesitate to put the stamp "healthy" on Asian finger food. But is sushi really healthy? To clarify this question, we have to take a closer look at the different components of rice rolls and their ingredients:

# RAW FISH

The typical main ingredients for sushi are raw fish or seafood, including, for example, tuna, salmon, freshwater eel, mackerel, shrimp and crab meat. These sea creatures are rich in high-quality animal protein, which humans need for various metabolic processes and building up the body's own proteins.

Iodine, a component of thyroid hormones, and some vitamins are also included. So fish is one of the main dietary sources of vitamin D. Mackerel and salmon in particular can have a high vitamin D content.

Fish is also an important supplier of omega-3 fatty acids: the fatty acids are present in high concentrations in the brain and nerve cells and reduce the risk of cardiovascular diseases.

# RICE

White rice grains are used in combination with a vinegar mixture, sugar and salt to prepare sushi rice. White rice is the grain that was ground and polished after harvesting - but it hardly contains any vitamins, minerals and fiber.

Since white rice is easier and faster to digest than, for example, brown rice, the blood sugar level rises rapidly after consumption and drops again just as quickly - cravings can be the result. Refined carbohydrates, such as white rice, are suspected of increasing the risk of type 2 diabetes or heart problems.

# NORI SHEETS

Hardly any sushi roll can do without nori algae. They keep the delicious filling together and are full of important nutrients. In addition to vitamins A, C, E and B 12, nori sheets provide zinc and some iodine.

They are also fat-free and rich in protein and satiating fiber. Their ingredients can lower blood cholesterol and have an anti-carcinogenic effect.

But if you now hope for a real nutrient bomb, you're wrong: Only a small amount of the algae is needed and processed for the delicious sushi specialties. For an adequate nutrient supply, the rice rolls alone play only a subordinate role.

## SOY SAUCE

Maki, nigiri and sashimi are dipped in soy sauce. For sushi fans, however, it is important to know that the traditionally produced soy sauce contains valuable ingredients: it contains certain amino acids and a lot of protein, but only a few calories and no fat.

US researchers also found that dark soy sauce contains about ten times as many antioxidants as red wine. To use this effect, one would have to drink soy sauce by the glass - the usual consumption amounts are hardly sufficient to bring verifiable health benefits.

Some experts also warn that one should think of the salt content in soy sauce, which averages 13 percent. As a natural seasoning, soy sauce is definitely more recommended and healthier than pure salt.

## WASABI

Without this hot and green spice, almost nothing works in Japan: wasabi. Incidentally, the widely used term "Japanese horseradish" is wrong: botanically speaking, there is no relationship between horseradish and wasabi.

In addition to the dried leaves, the root of the plant is mainly used to make the popular paste. The mustard oil glycosides, which are abundant in the wasabi, are among the phytochemicals that lower the risk of cancer and have an antibacterial and anti-inflammatory effect.

# SUSHI SAUCES

# SOY SESAME HONEY SAUCE

## INGREDIENTS FOR 1 PORTIONS

- 4 tbsp of soy sauce
- 1 teaspoon of sesame
- 1 teaspoon of honey, liquid

## PREPARATION

Total time approx. 2 minutes

1. Mix all the ingredients together and taste best according to your personal needs.

# JAPANESE SAUCE

## INGREDIENTS FOR 2 PORTIONS

- 1 teaspoon of olive oil
- 1 small onion
- 3 toes garlic
- 10 g of ginger, fresh
- 50 ml soy sauce
- 80 g sugar

## PREPARATION

Total time approx. 10 minutes

1. Peel the onion and cut it into small cubes. Peel the garlic and ginger and also finely dice. Fry everything together in the heated olive oil until everything is golden yellow. Add soy sauce and sugar and simmer for another 5-7 minutes. Finally, filter the sauce and only use the pure sauce.

# TERIYAKI SAUCE

## INGREDIENTS FOR 1 PORTIONS

- 4 tbsp. of soy sauce
- 1 tbsp. of rice wine
- Garlic cloves
- 2 teaspoons of ginger, grated
- 1 teaspoon of salt

## PREPARATION

Total time approx. 10 minutes

1. Mix all ingredients, garlic pressed, well.
2. This sauce is well suited for marinating meat (recipe information is sufficient for approx. 500 g).
3. Instead of rice wine, sherry can also be used.

# SUSHI SAUCE

## INGREDIENTS FOR 1 PORTIONS

- 3 tbsp. of soy sauce, dark
- 3 tbsp. of vinegar (sushi - vinegar)
- 4 tbsp. of water
- 1 tbsp. of sugar
- 1 pinch of salt
- 5 drops of oil (sesame oil)
- 0.33 g of bell pepper, red

## PREPARATION

Total time approx. 15 minutes

1.  Put all other ingredients apart from the peppers in a high container and whisk. Clean the peppers, cut them into very small cubes and add them. Stir again and let steep for a few hours until ready to eat.

# SUSHI RECIPES

# QUICK SUSHI RICE

## INGREDIENTS FOR 4 PORTIONS

- 250 g of rice (sushi - rice)
- 2 tbsp of vinegar (rice vinegar)
- 1 tbsp of sugar
- 1 teaspoon of salt

## PREPARATION

Total time approx. 20 minutes

1. Rinse sushi rice in a colander under running cold water until the water runs clear and let the kernels drain well.
2. Bring the rice to the boil with 300 ml of water, let it boil for 2 minutes, reduce the heat and cover and let the rice swell over low heat for 10 minutes.
3. Remove the lid, clamp 2 layers of kitchen paper between the pot and lid and let the rice cool for another 10 to 15 minutes.
4. In the meantime, bring rice vinegar, salt and sugar to the boil and let them cool down again.
5. Put the rice in a bowl, drizzle the vinegar over it and work in with a wooden spatula, but do not stir.
6. Cover the rice with a damp cloth until further use.

# SUSHI RICE

## INGREDIENTS FOR 4 PORTIONS

- 450 g of rice, california short grain rice (nishiki)
- 600 ml of water

Also: (for the spice mix for sushi rice)

- 100 ml of rice vinegar
- 2 tbsp of sugar
- 1 teaspoon of salt
- 4 drops of soy sauce

# PREPARATION

Total time approx. 1 hour 25 minutes

1. Wash rice thoroughly in a sieve until the water remains clear, then drain well.

2. Put the rice with the specified amount of water in the pot and let it rest for about 20 minutes.

3. Then close the pot with a well-fitting lid and slowly warm the contents. Then set the heat to the highest level and bring to a boil.

4. Now put it back on the smallest setting and let the rice swell for about 10 minutes.

5. Take the pot off the stove, put a folded kitchen towel under the lid and let the rice swell for another 10 minutes.

6. Mix the seasoning ingredients in a saucepan and heat until the sugar and salt have completely dissolved.

7. Then pour the seasoning mixture over the rice and mix together. (Warning, there is now rice vinegar that has already been seasoned with salt and sugar, then simply pour the "finished" vinegar over the rice with a dash of soy sauce!)

8. Let the rice cool well. The rice can then be processed into sushi. If the rice is only processed later, it is advisable to cover it with a damp cloth so that it does not dry out.

# TEMAKI

## INGREDIENTS FOR 1 PORTIONS

- Rice, sushi finished
- 2 nori sheets
- Wasabi paste
- 2 tbsp of rice vinegar
- 250 ml of water

For the filling:

- 2 carrots cut into fine strips
- 1 cucumber, cut into fine strips
- 200 g of salmon, cut into thin strips
- 200 g of tuna cut into thin strips
- 1 pack of surimi, cut into short sticks
- Cress
- Soy sauce
- Ginger pickled

# PREPARATION

Total time approx. 30 minutes

1. Mix vinegar and water in a small bowl.

2. Halve a nori sheet in the middle.

3. Immerse your hands in the vinegar water so that the rice does not stick to it.

4. Put a heaped tablespoon of sushi rice in the left half of the seaweed leaf. Spread the rice and spread a little wasabi paste on it.

5. Arrange different fillings diagonally on the rice. They should point to the top left corner of the Nori sheet.

6. Fold the lower left corner to the upper right corner of the nori sheet. Roll up the sheet further into a bag. Glue a grain of rice in the bottom right corner and fasten the corner to the bag.

7. Arrange several sushi bags in a glass or bowl and serve with soy sauce and pickled ginger.

# SASHIMI ON POINTED CABBAGE SALAD

## INGREDIENTS FOR 4 PORTIONS

- 400 g of salmon, or sushi-quality tuna
- 1 small head of pointed cabbage, about 300g
- Spring onion
- 3 tsp of ginger, pickled sushi
- 1 ½ m in size lemon, the juice
- ½ lemon, cut into 4 slices
- 2 teaspoons of sesame oil
- 4 tsp of soy sauce, light
- 3 tsp of horseradish
- 1 teaspoon of honey
- Salt and pepper
- 2 discs of toast
- 4 tsp of caviar, (trout caviar)
- 2 tbsp of sesame
- 2 tbsp of butter
- Wasabi paste

# PREPARATION

Total time approx. 2 hours

1.  First grate the cabbage roughly and remove the stalk if necessary. Then cut the spring onions into very fine rings and mix with the grated cabbage.

2.  Now cut 3 heaped teaspoons of sushi ginger into small pieces and add them to pointed cabbage.

3.  The dressing for the pointed cabbage salad is mixed from the lemon juice, the sesame oil, the soy sauce, the horseradish and the bee honey and added about 1 hour before consumption.

4.  Now 2 slices of toast are cut into small cubes and toasted with the butter until golden brown.

5.  At the same time, the sesame seeds are roasted in a coated pan (without additives).

6.  Shortly before serving, you should season the cabbage salad with salt and pepper. It should have a good sour note and a strong horseradish aroma.

7.  Now put one serving of salad (a small cup full) per person on the middle of the plate. Each portion is topped with about 100 g of salmon or tuna in thin strips. As a decorative "crown", place a teaspoon of trout caviar on the pointed cabbage sashimi portion and frame it with the toasted bread cubes. Now only sprinkle the raw fish with the roasted sesame seeds and add a slice of lemon with a dab of wasabi paste and serve immediately.

# NIGIRI

## INGREDIENTS FOR 1 PORTIONS

- 1 port. of rice, sushi finished
- Wasabi paste
- 200 g of salmon, cut into thin strips
- 200 g of tuna cut into thin strips
- Mackerel, cut into thin strips
- Radish, japanese, pickled
- Rice vinegar
- Water
- Soy sauce
- Pickled ginger

# PREPARATION

Total time approx. 30 minutes

1. Mix vinegar and water in a small bowl and dip your hands in it so that the rice does not stick to them.

2. Roll a chicken-sized amount of rice between your palms to create an oval. Place on the work surface and make several such rice balls. Place the toppings in front of the rice balls and spread a little wasabi paste on each rice ball.

3. Place the topping on the rice oval and press down gently.

4. Arrange on a plate and serve with soy sauce and pickled ginger.

# SAKE NIGIRI (SALMON)

## INGREDIENTS FOR 1 PORTIONS

- 1 cup of rice, (sushi rice)
- 200 g of sliced salmon (wild salmon, smoked)
- 200 g of cream cheese, with herbs
- 1 bunch radish
- 1 tbsp of soy sauce, (light)
- 1 tbsp of sugar
- ½ tsp of salt

For the set:
- Dill flags
- Chives - stalks

# PREPARATION

Total time approx. 20 minutes

1. The ingredients are enough for 12 salmon rolls.

2. Cook the rice according to the package, stirring in salt, sugar and soy sauce and then set aside.

3. Clean, wash and finely chop the radishes.

4. Spread the salmon slices slightly overlapping on a work surface covered with foil so that a closed rectangle of approx. 30 x 22 cm is created. Then spread the rice, then the cream cheese on top. Sprinkle the radishes over it and roll up the salmon with the foil and place in the freezer for about 30 minutes.

5. Then take out, cut into approx. 2 cm wide slices, arrange on a plate and garnish with dill flags and chives.

# EBI NIGIRI (SHRIMPS)

## INGREDIENTS FOR 4 PORTIONS

- Rice (sushi - rice), recipe in my profile, half of it
- 8 shrimps - raw, unpeeled tails
- 2 teaspoons of horseradish (wasabi powder)
- 4 tablespoons of water
- 2 tbsp of vinegar (rice vinegar)
- 2 teaspoons of rice wine (mirin)
- Salt
- Soy sauce
- Ginger pickled

# PREPARATION

Total time approx. 35 minutes

1.  Wash the prawn tails and cook over low heat in boiling salted water for 4 to 5 minutes. Take out and quench in ice water.

2.  Mix the wasabi powder with 2-4 tablespoons of water and let it swell. Remove the prawns from the shells, except for the tail segment. Remove the dark intestine from the back. Slit open from the abdomen, but not completely. They should be connected by about 1 cm on each side.

3.  Mix rice vinegar and rice wine in a deep plate, turn the prawns inside and let them steep for 2 minutes. Lift out, dab lightly and bend the two halves into a ring. Coat the inside with wafer-thin wasabi paste.

4.  With moistened hands, shape 1 tablespoon of sushi rice into an elongated dumpling and press the top slightly flat. Place the prawns on the rice pillows and gently press them down. Press on the sushi with the shrimps.

5.  Serve with soy sauce, remaining wasabi paste for dipping and pickled ginger.

# NIGIRI (SMOKED SALMON)

## INGREDIENTS FOR 4 PORTIONS

- 420 g of rice (sushi rice)
- 300 g of smoked salmon
- Spice paste (wasabi)
- Soy sauce
- Ginger, sweet and sour

## PREPARATION

Total time approx. 10 minutes

1. For those who don't really like raw fish. The preparation for sushi rice can be found in the CK database.

2. Cut the salmon into 5 cm long and 3 cm wide strips, dampen hands with water and take about 2 tablespoons of sushi rice and shape them into a 5-6 cm long, rectangular block with rounded sides and corners. Then cover the rice with the salmon strips and shape everything appetizing again.

3. Mix the soy sauce with the wasabi paste (caution spicy) according to taste, add ginger.

# SURIMI MAKI

## INGREDIENTS FOR 2 PORTIONS

- 1 port of rice (sushi rice), prepared
- 1 pack of surimi
- ½ avocado
- 2 tbsp of cream cheese
- Nori sheets

## PREPARATION

Total time approx. 30 minutes

1. Core and peel the avocado, then cut long strips, about 5 x 5 mm thin. Halve or quarter the surimi, depending on the size.
2. Place the nori sheet on a bamboo mat so that the lower side of the nori sheet lies on the lower edge of the mat. Spread the rice about 7mm thick over 2/3 of the nori sheet. Now spread a tablespoon of cream cheese about 3 cm wide in the middle of the rice. Place the avocado and surimi strips on each, about 3 to 4 strips each. Then carefully roll up with even pressure. This results in pretty thick maki rolls. Brush the roll with a little water or rice vinegar / water mixture (this makes it easier to cut). Cut off the ends, cut the roll into pleasant pieces, at least 1.5 cm long.

# SAKE MAKI (SALMON)

## INGREDIENTS FOR 2 PORTIONS

- 250 g of rice (sushi rice)
- 375 ml of water
- 1 tbsp of rice vinegar
- ½ tbsp of mirin
- ½ tbsp of sugar
- 1 teaspoon of salt
- 6 nori sheets
- 250 g of salmon steak, in the pan from both sides for 8 min. Fried and cut into strips
- 1 teaspoon of wasabi paste
- 6 cm salad cucumber, with skin, cut into thin strips
- ½ bell pepper, red, cut into thin strips

# PREPARATION

Total time approx. 45 minutes

1. Wash the rice in a sieve under running water until the draining water is clear. Bring the rice to a boil with the water in a saucepan, reduce the heat considerably and cook the rice for 10-12 minutes. In the meantime, mix the rice vinegar with mirin, sugar and salt in a small bowl until everything is completely dissolved. Put the rice in a flat bowl (no metal!) And let it cool for 10 minutes. Add the rice vinegar solution and carefully fold in with a wooden spoon. Let cool completely and divide into 6 equal portions.

2. Now place a nori sheet with the glossy side down on a bamboo mat and spread 1 rice portion thinly and evenly on it; Leave a 1.5 cm margin at one end. Use a spoon to make a furrow in the front third across the direction of the roll and apply wasabi paste. Be careful, wasabi is pretty hot! Then put the fried salmon strips in the furrow and place cucumber strips and / or pepper strips behind them as you like. Moisten the free end of the nori sheet with a little water. Now raise the bamboo mat at the front a little and lift the nori sheet around the filling under gentle pressure. Raise the bamboo mat further while rolling in the sushi roll until it is completely closed. You have to practice that a couple of times. For me it worked quite well the first time!

3. In the end there are 6 pretty sushi rolls in front of you, waiting for the final maki shape. Now it's time to prepare the tool, meaning to make a good knife ultra-sharp. Otherwise the maki sushi look more like car tires! Place a sushi roll on a wooden board and cut the ends clean straight (the remains are for the cook!). Always immerse the knife in cold water before each further cutting! Divide the sushi roll in the middle and cut each half into 4 equal maki sushi. Arrange on a large plate with the cut surface facing up. Cool the finished sushi or consume it immediately.

4. Set the table, prepare sushi sashimi sauce, wasabi paste and pickled ginger and enjoy piece by piece!

# TEKKA MAKI (TUNA)

## INGREDIENTS FOR 1 PORTIONS

- 1 can of tuna in water
- 5 tbsp of mayonnaise
- Salt
- Pepper
- Nori sheets
- 100 g of rice, (sushi rice)
- Sugar
- Rice wine

# PREPARATION

Total time approx. 1 hour

1.  Wash out the sushi rice. This means running water over it until only clear water is left.

2.  Then cook according to the package instructions. Put 1/2 teaspoon of sugar in 2 tablespoons of rice wine vinegar and heat. Stir the warm vinegar slowly under the still warm, cooked rice.

3.  Mix the tuna with the mayo and salt and pepper and season to taste.

4.  For the tuna sushi, place a nori sheet (with the smooth side) on a bamboo mat and spread the adhesive rice thinly on it so that approx. 3/4 of the sheet is covered with rice. A small margin should be left at the top and bottom. In the middle comes a narrow strip with the prepared tuna.

5.  Roll everything up and put in the fridge for a few minutes. Then cut the sushi roll and sushi pieces with a lightly dampened and sharp knife.

6.  Ginger, wasabi and teriyaki sauce can also be served.

# KIMCHI MAKI

## INGREDIENTS FOR 3 PORTIONS

- 100 ml of sushi rice
- 1 tbsp of sesame oil, dark
- 1 tbsp of rice vinegar
- 1 tbsp of sesame
- 1 teaspoon of salt
- Spring onion, green part
- 1 pack of nori sheets
- 6 tbsp of kimchi

# PREPARATION

Total time approx. 1 hour 5 minutes

1. Cook the rice with double the amount of water over medium heat. Add a little more water if necessary. Let the rice cool and then stir in the sesame oil, rice vinegar, sesame seeds and salt.

2. Spread 2 tablespoons of rice on the lower half of the nori leaf and add a row of spring onions and 2 tablespoons of kimchi. Roll up and dampen the end with water to make it stick better.

3. Place the sushi roll with the seam facing down on a wooden board. Do the same with the other two Nori sheets. Finally cut the rolls into 1.5 - 2 cm thick slices and serve with a little soy sauce.

# SUSHI ROLLS

## INGREDIENTS FOR 2 PORTIONS

- 1 cup of rice (sushi rice)
- Horseradish (wasabi)
- Nori sheets
- Carrot
- 100 g of meat from crayfish
- 100 g of shrimp
- Salmon, pickled
- Soy sauce
- Pickled ginger
- Spring onions

# PREPARATION

Total time approx. 1 hour 30 minutes

1. Soak the sushi rice in the water for about 15 minutes, then let it boil. For a cup of rice you need about 1.5 cups of water. There is also precise instructions on the rice pack.

2. In the meantime, the shrimps can be prepared using a steam cooker and briefly scalding. Peel the carrots and cut them into thin strips. The same goes for the spring onions.

3. Now place one of the nori sheets on a kitchen towel and apply the rice, which has now cooled down, 1 cm from the edge. Cover the leaf not too thickly but evenly. Now spread a little bit of the wasabi on top. Attention! The stuff is sharp. Then spread the shrimp approximately in the middle and parallel to the lower margin of the nori. Add strips of spring onion and carrot in the middle as required.

4. Moisten the exposed edge and wrap a roll using a kitchen towel. Press firmly ... Done! .... Cut the roll into slices in the refrigerator and shortly before serving.

5. A bowl of soy sauce and the pickled ginger are served.

6. Do the same for the crab meat and salmon.

# THIN SUSHI ROLLS

## INGREDIENTS FOR 1 PORTIONS

- 500 g of rice, finished sushi
- 1 can of wasabi paste
- 1 point of nori sheets

For the filling:

- Cucumber
- Carrot
- 200 g of salmon fillet, skinned
- 200 g of fish fillet, (tuna fillet)
- Radish, japanese, pickled
- Avocado
- 2 tbsp of rice vinegar
- 250 ml of water
- Soy sauce
- Pickled ginger

# PREPARATION

Total time approx. 30 minutes

1. Depending on your taste, choose the filling and cut the vegetables into chopsticks approx. 1 cm thick and the fish into pieces as thick as pencils.

2. Mix rice vinegar and water in a small bowl.

3. Place a bamboo mat on the work surface. Fold a nori sheet in half and break apart. Place the glossy, smooth side of the nori sheet half down on the bamboo mat.

4. Dip your hands in the vinegar water so that the rice does not stick to it. Take a handful of rice and form an elongated block.

5. Place the rice in the middle of the nori sheet and spread it evenly with your fingertips. Leave a 1 cm wide strip at the top.

6. Brush the rice in the middle with a little wasabi paste, do not overdo it, the wasabi taste should not overlap that of the ingredients.

7. Place a strip of fish or vegetables on the wasabi-coated rice. Raise the front end of the bamboo mat and slowly roll it up.

8. Roll up so far that the end of the nori sheet meets the edge of the rice. Apply light pressure to shape the roll.

9. Now only the free Nori strip looks out. Carefully shape the roll with both hands. Set the sushi roll aside and form the remaining rolls.

10. Dip a paper towel in the vinegar water and use it to wipe a sharp knife with a damp cloth. Halve the rolls with the knife.

11. Moisten the blade with the cloth after each cut. Place both roll halves in a row and cut twice so that 6 pieces of the same size are made. Arrange on a plate and serve with soy sauce and pickled ginger.

# THICK SUSHI ROLLS

## INGREDIENTS FOR 1 PORTIONS

- 500 g of rice, finished sushi
- 1 pack of nori sheets
- Wasabi paste

For the filling:

- Carrot cut into thin strips
- Cucumber, cut into thin strips
- 200 g of salmon or tuna cut into pencil-sized chopsticks
- Radish, japanese, pickled
- 1 pack of beans, green, cut into small pieces and steamed
- Avocado, cut into thin strips
- Tofu bags cut into 1 cm thick strips
- 2 tbsp of rice vinegar
- 250 ml of water
- Soy sauce
- Pickled ginger

# PREPARATION

Total time approx. 45 minutes

1.  Depending on your taste, choose the filling and cut the vegetables into chopsticks approx. 1 cm thick and the fish into pieces as thick as pencils.

2.  Mix rice vinegar and water in a small bowl. Place a bamboo mat on the work surface. Place a nori sheet on the bamboo mat with the glossy, smooth side down.

3.  Dip your hands in the vinegar water so that the rice does not stick to it. Take a handful of rice and form an elongated block.

4.  Place 2 blocks of rice in the middle of the nori sheet and spread them evenly with your fingertips. Leave a 4 cm wide strip free at the top. Brush the rice in the middle with a little wasabi paste, do not overdo it, the wasabi taste should not overlap that of the ingredients.

5.  Place a strip of fish on the wasabi-coated rice. Frame with vegetable strips on both sides. Raise the front end of the bamboo mat and slowly roll it up. Hold the filling with your middle, ring and little finger in place.

6.  Roll up so far that the end of the nori sheet meets the edge of the rice. Apply light pressure to shape the roll.

7.  Now only the Free Nori Strip looks out. Carefully shape the roll with both hands. Set the sushi roll aside and form the remaining rolls.

8.  Dip a tea towel in the vinegar water and use it to wipe a sharp knife with a damp cloth. Halve the rolls with the knife.

9.  Moisten the blade with the cloth after each cut. Place both roll halves in a row and cut twice so that 6 pieces of the same size are created. Arrange on a plate and serve with soy sauce and pickled ginger.

# MUSHROOM SUSHI ROLLS

## INGREDIENTS FOR 4 PORTIONS

- 3 cups of round grain rice
- 0.33 cups of rice vinegar
- 3 tbsp of sugar
- 1 teaspoon of salt, painted
- 8 shiitake mushrooms, dried, for the filling
- 0.33 cups of water (shiitake soaking water)
- 0.67 cups of dashi (1 pinch of instant fish broth dissolved in 0.66 cups of water)
- 1½ tbsp of sugar
- ½ tbsp of sake (japanese rice wine) or white wine
- 1 tbsp of soy sauce
- 1 egg
- 1 teaspoon of sugar
- 1 pinch salt
- Oil, for frying
- 100 g of spinach leaves
- Nori leaves (seaweed leaves)
- Soy sauce for dipping

# PREPARATION

Total time approx. 1 hour 30 minutes

1. Boil the rice and put it in a bowl (ideally an untreated wooden bowl that can absorb excess water).

2. While the rice is cooking, stir the vinegar dressing (vinegar, sugar, salt) until the sugar has dissolved. It is best to warm up briefly.

3. Pour the vinegar dressing over the rice and mix well with a wooden spoon. Then let it cool down.

4. Soak the shiitake mushrooms in a bowl with lukewarm water for approx. 20 min. Drain and store the soaking water. Cut mushrooms into 7 - 8 mm wide strips.

5. Boil the mushrooms together with the ingredients water to soy sauce in a small saucepan and cook over low heat until the excess liquid has evaporated.

6. Beat the 3 eggs, whisk the sugar to salt with ingredients and strain through a tea strainer. Heat a little oil in a pan and bake a thick pancake from the entire (!) Dough. Let it cool and cut into strips about 1 cm long.

7. Blanch the spinach leaves, quench in cold water and wring out well.

8. Place Nori on a bamboo mat with the smooth side down. Spread about a quarter of the sushi rice evenly with wet hands. Leave about 1 cm of the Nori sheet free at the front.

9. Spread a quarter of the spinach, ice cream strips and mushrooms in the middle of the nori sheet.

10. Shape a firm roll using the bamboo mat. Then press them down with your fingers and shape them.

11. Do the same with the remaining ingredients. Cut each of the 4 sushi rolls into about 8 slices.

12. Dip in soy sauce before eating.

# FISH AND CHIPS SUSHI ROLLS

## INGREDIENTS FOR 4 PORTIONS

- 500 g of sushi rice or good milk rice
- 4 tbsp of powder (sushi vinegar powder "sushinoko")
- 8 fish fingers with white meat
- 200 g of french fries, frozen
- 4 nori sheets
- Mayonnaise
- Ketchup

# PREPARATION

Total time approx. 50 minutes

1. Sushi vinegar powder is available in the Asian shop. Alternatively, the sushi rice can also be cooked with sushi vinegar, choosing a recipe from the database.

2. Pre-heat the oven to 220 degrees Celsius. Wash the rice 2 or 3 times in a saucepan, then drain the water. Put 700 ml of cold water in the saucepan and let the rice rest for 10 minutes. Please make sure that the pot holds more than 1.8 l and has a blanket!

3. Place baking paper on the baking sheet, spread the fries and fish sticks on top and slide the baking sheet into the oven. It takes about 20 minutes for fries and fish sticks to be ready.

4. Now cook the rice. To do this, place the saucepan on an electric stove at maximum setting (3) and wait until foam comes out of the saucepan. It takes about 10 to 15 minutes. Then turn the heat to zero and leave the pan on the stove for 15 minutes. Please note that the size of the pot may prevent the foam from coming out. To avoid stuck rice, check from time to time - but not often! - Whether there is still liquid. When the liquid has been used up, turn the heat to zero immediately and leave the pan on the stove for 15 minutes. When the rice is ready, put the rice in a bowl and mix in the sushi vinegar powder. This will make the rice smooth.

5. Take the fish fingers and fries out of the oven when they're done

6. Now the roll comes. There are several tips for this, but my recommendation is to wrap a bamboo mat with cling film so that the rice doesn't stick to the mat.

7. Place on the mat of nori leaves and spread the rice on top. Spread 2 fish sticks and French fries on the rice and add majo and ketchup on top. Shape everything into a roll using the bamboo mat.

# BUCKWHEAT SUSHI ROLLS

## INGREDIENTS FOR 2 PORTIONS

- 200 g of buckwheat
- Rice vinegar
- Sugar
- 1 teaspoon flour, dissolved in cold water
- Nori sheets
- 150 g of smoked salmon
- 400 g of mixed vegetables, e.g. Carrot, cucumber, avocado, bell pepper, asparagus, radish, ...
- 4 tbsp of soy sauce
- 2 tsp of wasabi powder
- 2 tsp of pickled ginger

# PREPARATION

Total time approx. 1 hour 20 minutes

1.  Boil the buckwheat in double the amount of water for 20 minutes. Salt the water if necessary. Then leave the buckwheat covered for 20 minutes and mix in some rice vinegar and sugar. Then add the flour or starch dissolved in water and heat again. Stir in the buckwheat. It should have a sticky consistency.

2.  After it has cooled a little, spread the buckwheat as a thin layer on a nori sheet, which lies on a bamboo mat. The edges should be left a little free. Then place the desired contents, i.e. vegetables and fish, in the middle of the length of the coated sheet and roll it up using the bamboo mat and press firmly together. Knowledge of sushi and practice are almost essential here. Now cut the pieces down with a sharp knife wetted with vinegar. The edge pieces can be tried on this occasion.

3.  Divide the soy sauce, the wasabi and the ginger into 2 portions, put them in separate bowls and serve with the buckwheat sushi. The soy sauce is used for short dipping, the wasabi for careful spreading and the ginger between the sushi pieces for "neutralizing", refreshing and snacking.

# CRISPY BIG SUSHI ROLLS

## INGREDIENTS FOR 2 PORTIONS

- Raw salmon
- Carrot
- Cucumber
- Avocado
- Philadelphia
- 5 Nori sheets
- Rice (sushi rice)
- Breadcrumbs
- Fat for the pan

# PREPARATION

Total time approx. 45 minutes

1. Cook the sushi rice as usual (possibly take a recipe from the database). Peel the carrots and cut lengthways into quarters. Cut the cucumber into 1 - 1 1/2 cm strips. Let the carrot and cucumber strips cool in the pan with a little water, briefly steam the sugar and salt. Cut the salmon lengthways into strips as well as the avocado.

2. Now cover the nori sheet with sushi rice. Place the ingredients for the filling in the first third and spread some of the cream cheese lengthways (preferably along the salmon). Now brush the not yet cut sushi roll with a little whisked egg white and roll through the breadcrumbs. Fry immediately in the hot pan with a little (!) Fat (not too long, so that the fish doesn't cook, it's really very quick)

3. Dab on kitchen paper and cut into slices. With soy sauce, pickled ginger and Thai chili sauce it tastes particularly good! The recipe can also be supplemented with surimi and pickled mustard cabbage.

# CAULIFLOWER SUSHI ROLLS

## INGREDIENTS FOR 3 PORTIONS

- 700 g of cauliflower,
- 150 ml of water, cold
- 1 g of guar gum
- 2 tbsp of rice vinegar
- Sweetener of your choice (e.g. 1 tbsp sukrin)
- Salt
- 5 nori sheets

For the filling:

- Shrimp and / or avocado, salmon, cucumber
- Wasabi paste

# PREPARATION

Total time approx. 40 minutes

1.  Wash the cauliflower and cut it into pieces, grate it in the food processor and boil it with about ¼ l water for 5-10 minutes. Drain and squeeze through a clean tea towel. Mix 1 g guar gum with 150 ml cold water. Put the cauliflower back in the pot or in a bowl and mix well with the sukrin, rice vinegar, salt and guar water mix until a thick porridge has formed.

2.  Place the nori sheets on the sushi mat, spread the cauliflower porridge about ½ cm thick and then topping with z. Shrimp, avocado, salmon and cucumber, brush with a little wasabi paste and then roll in, press well, leave something to stand and then cut into pieces with a damp, sharp knife.

# EGG SUSHI ROLLS

## INGREDIENTS FOR 2 PORTIONS

- 1 big egg
- Seasoned salt
- Salt and pepper
- 2 teaspoons of cream cheese
- 3 discs of smoked salmon, or other fish, whether or not raw
- 3 sheets of nori sheets
- Vegetables, e.g. Avocado, cucumber, carrots
- Soy sauce
- Wasabi paste
- Ginger root, inlaid

# PREPARATION

Total time approx. 35 minutes

1. Mix egg white, egg, pepper, salt, fry on both sides and halve to an omelet.

2. Cut the vegetables and salmon into thin strips.

3. Spread the nori sheets on a mat or baking paper and top with half of the omelette. Maybe the leaves still need to be cut. Brush the omelette with the cream cheese and top with vegetables and fish. Brush the ends of the leaves with water.

4. Roll the nori sheets tightly from one side to the other. Then cut the roll into two centimeters pieces, serve with soy sauce, wasabi and the pickled ginger.

# VEGAN SUSHI ROLLS

## INGREDIENTS FOR 4 PORTIONS

- 300 g of sushi rice
- 600 ml of water
- 60 ml of rice vinegar
- 1 teaspoon of sugar
- ½ tsp of salt
- 5 Nori sheets
- 1 small  salad cucumber, cut into strips
- 1 tomato cut into strips
- 1 small  avocado cut into strips

Furthermore:

- Soy sauce
- Wasabi

# PREPARATION

Total time approx. 50 minutes

1. Wash the sushi rice in a colander under cold running water until the water runs clear.

2. Then drain the sushi rice well.

3. Bring 600 ml of water to a boil in a saucepan, add the rice and reduce the heat, put the lid on and let it boil for 10 minutes. Remove the rice from the heat and cover with a dry, clean tea towel and let it evaporate for 10 to 15 minutes. Meanwhile heat the rice vinegar, dissolve the salt and sugar in it.

4. Put the rice in a bowl and add the rice vinegar and mix regularly with a wooden spatula and let cool.

5. Place a nori sheet on a sushi mat, spread 1 cm of rice on top, leaving a strip at the top. Place the cleaned and cut vegetables in the middle. Roll up the nori sheet evenly, then gently press the sushi into the bamboo mat until it has a slightly rectangular shape. This takes practice.

6. Cut the sushi into slice-wide slices with a sharp knife and serve with soy sauce and wasabi.

7. Other seasonal raw vegetables can also be used for the filling.

# VEGAN SUSHI DELUXE

## INGREDIENTS FOR 2 PORTIONS

- ½ cup of sushi rice
- 2 tbsp of rice vinegar (rice wine vinegar)
- ½ avocado
- ½ red pepper
- ½ carrot
- ¼ cucumber
- 4 nori sheets

Sausages, vegan (Merguez sausages)

- Wasabi paste
- Soy sauce

# PREPARATION

Total time approx. 50 minutes

1.  Put on the rice with twice the amount of water, bring to the boil briefly and then let it swell on a low flame for 15 minutes. Then remove from the heat, stir in the rice vinegar and let it cool down, otherwise the nori sheets will soak.

2.  Cut the avocado, bell pepper, carrot, cucumber and the sausage lengthways into thin chopsticks. Core the cucumber with a teaspoon before cutting.

3.  Place a nori sheet on the bamboo mat and cover the lower third with rice. Spread a strip of wasabi paste, the vegetable sticks and the merguez on top. Roll up firmly using the bamboo mat and cut the roll into several pieces using a damp, clean knife. Do the same with the other nori sheets.

4.  Serve the sushi with a bowl of soy sauce.

# VEGAN SPICY SUSHI ROLLS

## INGREDIENTS FOR 2 PORTIONS

- 4 nori sheets
- Chorizo, vegan
- ½ cup of sushi rice
- ½ bell pepper, red
- ½ avocado
- Salt
- Soy sauce

Also: (for the chipotle mayonnaise)

- 2 teaspoons of sauce (adobo sauce)
- Jalapeños (chipotle in adobo sauce)
- 50 ml of mayonnaise, vegan

# PREPARATION

Total time approx. 30 minutes

1. Cut the avocado, bell peppers and the sausage lengthways into thin strips. Place the rice with twice the amount of water and a pinch of salt, bring to the boil briefly and then let it swell on a low flame for 15 minutes until the water is completely boiled. Afterwards, let it cool down, otherwise the nori sheets will soak.

2. Place a nori sheet on the bamboo mat and cover the lower third with rice. Spread 2 teaspoons of chipotle mayonnaise on the rice. Then spread a row of vegetable sticks and chorizo on each. Roll up firmly using the bamboo mat and cut the roll into several pieces using a damp, clean knife. Do the same with the other nori sheets.

3. Serve the sushi with a bowl of soy sauce.

# VEGETABLE SUSHI ROLLS

## INGREDIENTS FOR 1 PORTIONS

- 70 g of sushi rice
- Salt
- 15 ml of rice vinegar
- 5 g of sugar
- 2 nori sheets
- 100 g of peas, frozen, or beans, white, cooked
- 50 g of soy quark (quark alternative)
- ½ tsp of wasabi powder
- 15 ml of soy sauce
- 1 small piece of ginger, fresher
- Garlic cloves
- Salt
- 1 pinch cayenne pepper
- 1½ of carrot, alternatively kohlrabi, beetroot, cucumber, peppers grated or cut into thin sticks,
- Spring onions
- Soy sauce
- Ginger

# PREPARATION

Total time approx. 50 minutes

1.  Place the sushi rice in a sieve and rinse thoroughly with water. Then the sushi rice in salted water with the lid closed over low heat for about 15 minutes. Simmer. Switch off the stove and the rice for another 5 min. let swell. Remove the lid, stir in the rice vinegar and sugar and let the sushi rice cool completely.

2.  In the meantime, puree the peas / beans with soy curd, wasabi powder, soy sauce, ginger and garlic to a creamy mass. Possibly. Season with salt and cayenne pepper.

3.  When the sushi rice has cooled completely, mix about 2/3 of the cream with the sushi rice.

4.  Wash, peel and prepare the vegetables ready for cooking (cut into thin strips, grate, etc.).

5.  Place the two nori sheets on the sushi mat with the rough side upwards with about 2 cm overlap. Spread the rice evenly over half of it evenly on the nori sheet. Top with the vegetables and the rest of the cream and use the sushi mat to gently roll them in with light pressure. At the end, leave about 2 cm of Nori sheet, moisten with water and seal the XXL roll.

# VEGETABLE SUSHI MIX

## INGREDIENTS FOR 1 PORTIONS

- 1 cup of rice (sushi or basmati rice)
- Water
- ½ carrot
- ¼ bell pepper, red
- Cucumber
- 1 teaspoon of wasabi powder or paste
- 1 shot of sake or dry white wine
- Rice vinegar
- 1 teaspoon of sugar
- Soy sauce, japanese
- Sesame oil or sunflower oil

# PREPARATION

Total time approx. 15 minutes

1.  First put the rice on according to the package instructions and let it simmer until there is no more water in the pot. In the meantime, wash the vegetables, peel the carrot and cucumber and cut everything into small, visually appealing pieces (diamonds, cubes, chopsticks ...).

2.  Heat the oil in a pan and add the carrots first, then the peppers and finally the cucumber and cook until firm. Then deglaze the whole thing with a little rice vinegar, sake and a dash of soy sauce (not too much of the soy sauce, otherwise the vegetables will turn brown). Sprinkle the sugar over it and let the liquid reduce.

3.  Now put the finished rice on a plate and spread the vegetables over it. Finally, mix wasabi with soy sauce (amount depending on taste) and drizzle over the dish.

# CHEESE SUSHI ROLLS

## INGREDIENTS FOR 2 PORTIONS

- 200 g of feta cheese
- 350 g of cream cheese, grainy
- ½ cucumber
- 150 g of smoked salmon
- 5 nori sheets
- Soy sauce, to taste

## PREPARATION

Total time approx. 35 minutes

1. Crumble the feta cheese and mix it carefully with the granular cream cheese. Cut the smoked salmon into strips. Peel the cucumber, scrape out the kernels inside with a spoon and cut the meat into long strips.
2. Place the nori sheet on the mat and brush 2/3 with the cheese paste (not too thick), put on a strip of smoked salmon and cucumber and roll it up like normal sushi. Let it rest a little so that the nori sheets can wet out, then cut into rolls about 3-4 cm long. Serve with soy sauce.

# TOFU SUSHI ROLLS

## INGREDIENTS FOR 5 PORTIONS

- 200 g of tofu, seasoned
- 200 g of arborio rice
- 100 g of bamboo shoot, inlaid
- 400 ml of water
- 200 ml of rice vinegar
- 10 pieces of nori sheets
- 4 tbsp of soy sauce
- 4 tbsp of oil (sunflower)

## PREPARATION

Total time approx. 30 minutes

1. Cut the tofu into elongated slices and fry in a pan with oil and soy sauce. Let cool down. Then briefly heat the seasoned tofu in the same pan.
2. Simmer the rice with the water until the water is absorbed (approx. 15 min.).
3. Spread the rice on the algae so that about 3/4 of the leaf is covered. Put in tofu and bamboo shoots. Roll up the algae leaves using a mat or a kitchen towel. Brush the last quarter with rice vinegar and glue the roll tightly with it.
4. Cut each roll into 5 pieces.

# AVOCADO SUSHI ROLLS

## INGREDIENTS FOR 2 PORTIONS

- 100 g of sushi rice
- 4 nori sheets
- 5 tbsp of rice vinegar
- 2 tbsp of sugar
- Salt
- Avocado

# PREPARATION

Total time approx. 55 minutes

1. You also need a makisu (bamboo mat) to make sushi.

2. First, the sushi rice is washed thoroughly until the water is clear. Then it is boiled in cold water, over medium heat for 15 min. long.

3. In the meantime you can mix and heat the rice vinegar with sugar and salt. When the rice is cooked, add the vinegar, stir and cover with a cotton cloth and 10 min. to let go.

4. Then wrap the bamboo mat with cling film and cut a nori sheet in half.

5. Halve an avocado, remove the peel and cut into slightly thicker slices.

6. Now spread the cooled rice on the nori sheet, leaving 1 cm free at the top and moistening this strip with water. Place the avocado in the middle and roll everything carefully with a little pressure. Finally, cut the roll into bite-size pieces.

7. Serve with wasabi, pickled ginger and soy sauce.

# SHIITAKE MUSHROOMS FOR SUSHI ROLLS

## INGREDIENTS FOR 2 PORTIONS

- 10 shiitake mushrooms, dried
- 2 tbsp of soy sauce
- 2 tbsp of sugar
- 2 teaspoons of mirin

# PREPARATION

Total time approx. 30 minutes

1.  The shiitake mushrooms are ideal for vegetarian sushi, e.g. shiitake cream cheese maki.

2.  Cover the dried shiitake mushrooms with boiling water and soak them for 15 minutes. Alternatively, you can also take cold water and soak it for an hour (this will make the mushroom aroma even more intense).

3.  Drain the mushrooms and collect the soaking water. If necessary, remove the hard stem ends. If the mushrooms are used for sushi, it is advisable to cut them into strips at this point.

4.  Cover the mushrooms in a saucepan with the soaking water and bring to a boil, then reduce the heat and simmer for 2 minutes. Add the sugar and soy sauce and simmer, stirring occasionally, until the liquid has completely evaporated.

5.  Finally add the mirin and stir. The last step is not absolutely necessary, but the mirin gives the mushrooms the finishing touch.

# SHIITAKE SUSHI ROLLS

## INGREDIENTS FOR 4 PORTIONS

- 4 mushrooms (shiitake), dried
- 2 tbsp of soy sauce, japanese
- 1 tbsp of sugar

## PREPARATION

Total time approx. 40 minutes

1. Soak mushrooms in hot water for about 20 minutes. Remove the stems and cut the heads into fine strips. Simmer in 1/2 cup of the soaking liquid together with the soy sauce and sugar until the liquid has almost evaporated. Let cool down.

2. Work the mushroom strips into maki sushi (rice inner rolls). They look very good in color (brown) as well as aromatic (sweet, umami, and sour) and form a nice contrast to vegetable strips.

# CAPRESE SUSHI ROLLS

## INGREDIENTS FOR 1 PORTIONS

- 2 nori sheets
- 1 port of rice (sushi rice), ready prepared, recipes in the database
- 1 ball of mozzarella
- Tomatoes
- Basil

## PREPARATION

Total time approx. 20 minutes

1. Halve the nori sheet lengthways. Place one half on the bamboo mat and cover with rice. Cut the mozzarella into small pencils. Wash the tomatoes and also cut them into sticks, first cut them into slices, cut out the inside and make the sticks out of the firm rim of the tomato. Wash the basil. Spread the tomato and mozzarella sticks on the rice, and the basil leaves as well. Form everything into a roll.

2. Do the same with the second half of the nori sheet.

# HERBAL MUSHROOM SUSHI ROLLS

## INGREDIENTS FOR 2 PORTIONS

- 300 g of herbal mushrooms
- 180 g of shirati rice noodles
- 2 tbsp of cream cheese
- 200 g of pak choi
- Spring onion
- Coriander
- 4 nori sheets

# PREPARATION

Total time approx. 40 minutes

1.  Slice the herb mushrooms lengthways and fry them in the pan with a little butter or oil. You can be a little tanned for the aroma. Let cool down.

2.  Cut the pak choi, if necessary cut the leaves lengthways and briefly fry in the pan over high heat. It should remain crisp.

3.  Clean the green from the spring onions and cut into strips.

4.  Wash the shirataki in a colander. If they smell fishy (due to the alkaline liquid), rinse them briefly with vinegar, then rinse the vinegar as well. Drain well and then mix with the cream cheese.

5.  Spread a third of each on a nori sheet, place 1/3 spring onions, 1/3 mushrooms and 1/3 pak choi lengthways on top. If you like coriander, you can sprinkle chopped coriander over it. Roll up and cut into slices.

6.  Serve with soy sauce and wasabi.

# CARROT AND CUCUMBER SUSHI ROLLS

## INGREDIENTS FOR 4 PORTIONS

- 500 g of rice pudding
- 5 tbsp of rice vinegar or brandy vinegar
- 4 carrots
- Cucumber
- 8 nori sheets
- Olive oil

# PREPARATION

Total time approx. 1 hour

1.  We thought about the variant with the milk rice, because we could not buy sushi rice. We think it tastes delicious too!

2.  Place the rice in the rice cooker and wash twice thoroughly with lukewarm water. Drain the water and smooth the rice a little. Then spread 2-3 tablespoons of rice vinegar on the rice. Pour the cooking water up to 2-3 finger-widths above the rice surface and cook the rice. When the rice cooker has switched off, leave the sushi rice covered for another 10 minutes. Then switch off the rice cooker completely and let the rice cool down. For this purpose, the lid can also be opened.

3.  The rice can also be prepared the evening before (if there is to be sushi for lunch). However, do not open the lid overnight, just switch off the cooker and let the rice cool down, otherwise the surface will become very dry and part of the rice will then no longer be usable.

4.  Wash, peel and quarter the carrots for the carrot sushi. Fry in a hot pan in plenty of olive oil for about 5 minutes, remove and place on a plate! Place the bamboo mat on a smooth surface and place a nori sheet on it. Then spread rice with a dough scraper approx. 3-5 mm thick over the entire surface of the leaf. Now place 2-3 slices of carrot 2 cm from the edge and form a roll. Depending on how thick you want the sushi to be later, the filling must be measured. A little feeling is required! Now cut the sushi roll into approx. 3 cm thick slices and arrange on a platter. 4 nori sheets are used for the carrot sushi, the other half for the cucumber sushi.

5.  Wash, peel the cucumber (possibly leave some peel), quarter lengthways and core. Then cut it again across the length of the nori sheet. Simmer the cucumber slices in a brew of water and 2 tablespoons of vinegar for about 5 minutes, also remove and place on a plate. Proceed as for the carrot sushi.

# SUSHI WITH CAULIFLOWER

## INGREDIENTS FOR 2 PORTIONS

- 1 gr of head cauliflower
- Salt
- 30 ml of rice vinegar
- 20 g of sugar (1 tbsp.)
- 1 teaspoon of oyster sauce
- 100 g of double cream cheese
- 100 g of salmon
- Cucumber
- Vegetables or fish of your choice
- 4 nori sheets
- Soy sauce
- Wasabi

# PREPARATION

Total time approx. 2 hours 44 minutes

1. Divide the cauliflower into florets and wash. Bring lightly salted water to a boil. Put the cauliflower in the boiling water and cook for 4 minutes, it should remain very firm to the bite. Drain well and let cool. Granulate with the food processor or blender.

2. Mix the vinegar with the sugar and the oyster sauce and heat briefly so that everything combines well. Then pour over the cauliflower and mix with the cream cheese to a mass.

3. Cut vegetables and fish into thin strips.

4. Maki:

5. Spread a cauliflower mass on a nori sheet. Leave the upper edge approx. 2 cm free. Spread a little wasabi on it if you like. Place the vegetable and fish strips lengthways in the middle. Moisten the edge with water so that it sticks better together. Now wrap it into a tight roll with a sushi mat. Chill the roll for an hour, then cut into pieces of equal size.

6. Nigiri:

7. Form small blocks by hand or with a nigiri form from the cauliflower mass. Brush with wasabi and top with fish. Chill for an hour too.

# CALIFORNIA ROLLS

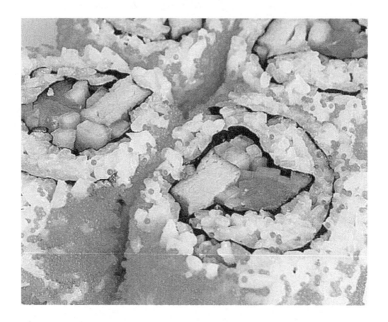

## INGREDIENTS FOR 1 PORTIONS

- 500 g of rice, sushi finished
- 1 pack of nori sheets
- Mayonnaise
- Wasabi paste
- 2 tbsp of rice vinegar
- 250 ml of water

For the filling:

- 1 pack of surimi
- Avocado, cut into thin strips
- Salad cucumber, cut into thin strips
- 50 g of roe from the fly fish
- Sesame, black and white
- Soy sauce
- Pickled ginger

# PREPARATION

Total time approx. 45 minutes

1. Mix rice vinegar and water in a small bowl.

2. Place a bamboo mat on the work surface and wrap in cling film. Fold a nori sheet in half and break apart. Place the halved nori sheet on the mat.

3. Dip your hands in the vinegar water so that the rice does not stick to it. Take a handful of rice and form an elongated block.

4. Place the rice in the middle of the nori sheet and spread it evenly with your fingertips. Lift the rice-covered nori leaf and turn it over quickly.

5. Place the imitation crab meat and the cucumber strips in the middle of the nori sheet, pull a narrow strip of mayonnaise, seasoned with wasabi, and place the avocado strips on top.

6. Lift the bamboo mat and hold the filling if necessary. Start rolling up. Squeeze the roll lightly and give it a rectangular shape with gentle pressure.

7. Roll the mat apart again. Spread the fries on the sushi roll and press gently with a spoon. Turn the roll over to cover the underside with roe.

8. Dip a tea towel in the vinegar water and use it to wipe a sharp knife with a damp cloth. Halve the rolls with the knife.

9. Moisten the blade with the cloth after each cut. Place both roll halves in a row and cut twice so that 6 pieces of the same size are made. Arrange on a plate and serve with soy sauce and pickled ginger.

# CALIFORNIA ROLLS - SALMON AND AVOCADO

## INGREDIENTS FOR 1 PORTIONS

- Avocado
- Nori sheets
- 350 g of rice (sushi), cooked
- 100 g of cream cheese
- 300 g of salmon fillet, very fresh
- Wasabi paste
- Ginger root, pickled
- Soy sauce

# PREPARATION

Total time approx. 30 minutes

1.  Peel the avocado, remove the core, cut into 12 strips about 7 cm long. Halve the algae leaves. Cover a bamboo mat with cling film. Approx. spread 120 g of rice on top, press well. Place 1/2 seaweed leaf on top, spread with 25 g cream cheese, spread 3 avocado strips on each. Roll up and press together using the mat. Take out the sushi. Cut salmon into thin, large (approx. 5 x 22 cm) pieces and wrap them around the sushi roll. Cut into 8 pieces. Process the remaining ingredients in the same way. Serve sushi with wasabi, ginger and soy sauce.

2.  Basic sushi rice recipe for approx. 500 g of cooked rice:

3.  Wash 350 g sushi rice (e.g. American short grain rice) until the water remains clear. Approx. Soak in cold water for 30 minutes and drain. Place in a saucepan with 500 ml of water and possibly 1 piece of seaweed and cook over a medium heat for about 15 minutes. Remove the kelp, pull the pot off the stove and let it swell for about 15 minutes. Mix in 3 tablespoons of rice vinegar, 2 tablespoons of sugar and salt with a wooden spoon while allowing the rice to cool.

# CALIFORNIA ROLLS INSIDE OUT

## INGREDIENTS FOR 12 PORTIONS

- 250 g of rice, sushi rice, ready made
- 5 nori sheets
- 40 g of surimi
- Salad cucumber, 2 strips, cut lengthways
- ½ avocado
- 1 teaspoon of lemon juice
- 4 tbsp of sesame
- 1 tbsp of horseradish (cream)

# PREPARATION

Total time approx. 20 minutes

1.  Roast the sesame seeds in a pan without fat until golden, let them cool on a flat plate. Pat the surimi sticks dry and cut in half lengthways. Wash the cucumber, cut in half lengthways and remove the seeds with a spoon, cut the length of 2 strips about 0.5 cm wide. Peel the avocado, cut lengthways into strips and immediately drizzle with lemon juice.

2.  Wrap the sushi mat completely with cling film. Place a nori sheet with the smooth side down on top and cover completely with half of the rice. Press the rice lightly and then turn it over with the nori sheet so that the rice lies on the transparent film.

3.  Spread half of the horseradish on the lower third of the nori sheet, spread half of the surimi sticks, cucumber sticks and avocados on each, and roll up the whole thing.

4.  Form a second roll from the remaining ingredients. Cut the rolls into 6 pieces and roll each piece in toasted sesame.

# CALIFORNIA SUSHI WRAPS

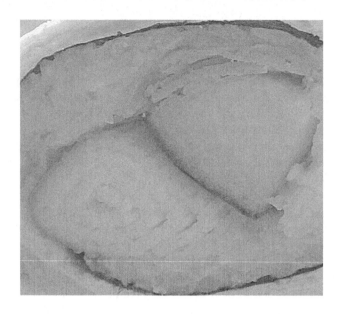

## INGREDIENTS FOR 4 PORTIONS

- 250 g of Rice (sushi rice)
- ½ tsp of salt
- 2 tbsp of Rice vinegar
- 1 bunch of Spring onions
- 4 Tortillas (wheat tortillas)
- 4 Nori sheets
- 2 Carrots
- 1 Cucumber
- 1 bag of Surimi sticks (8 sticks)
- Soy sauce

# PREPARATION

Total time approx. 1 day 30 minutes

1.  Cook the sushi rice according to the package instructions. Meanwhile, cut the spring onions into thin rings. Grate the carrots finely, peel, quarter and core the cucumber. Then mix the rice with salt, rice vinegar and spring onions and let cool.

2.  For each wrap, heat a tortilla in the microwave for 10 seconds. Place a nori sheet on the tortilla and spread 1/4 of the rice on top. Spread a thin layer of grated carrots on the rice. Place 1/4 of the cucumber and 2 surimis sticks on the edge of the wraps and start rolling up the wrap at this end. Wrap the ends about halfway through.

3.  Wrap each wrap very tightly with cling film and put in the fridge for 24 hours. Cut the wraps diagonally in the middle and serve with soy sauce.

# SUSHI MIX 1

## INGREDIENTS FOR 4 PORTIONS

- 450 g of rice (sushi rice)
- 1 avocado
- 1 cucumber
- 1 tbsp of mayonnaise
- 2 tbsp of sesame seeds, toasted
- 150 g of salmon
- 1 pack of surimi (crab meat imitation)
- 6 shrimps
- 150 g of tuna
- Wasabi paste (spicy japanese horseradish paste)
- Nori leaves (algae leaves)
- Pickled ginger (gari)
- Soy sauce
- Salad leaves, e.g. Lollo rosso

# PREPARATION

Total time approx. 45 minutes

Before you start, wrap the sushi mat with cling film, so the mat stays clean and the rice cannot stick in the spaces between the thin bamboo sticks.

### Maki with salmon

Take a nori sheet and cut it in half with a knife. Place the sheet on the bamboo mat with the rough side up so that the rice adheres better. Now lightly dampen the fingers in a bowl with water and spread a lot of cooled rice on the nori sheet so that the algae leaf is covered with rice, only a free edge should remain at the bottom so that the roll can be glued later. Now cut the salmon in stick form and place them lengthwise on the rice. Brush the salmon with wasabi, but only thinly, because wasabi is quite hot. Then moisten the uncovered edge of the nori sheet and, starting from the other side, fold in the bamboo mat so that a roll is created. If you press the rolled-up bamboo mat from above and from the sides, you get a square shape.

### California Roll or Inside-Out

Take half a sheet of algae, place it on the front area of the mat and cover the rough side completely with rice, sprinkle sesame on the rice. Take the free side of the bamboo mat, fold over the algae leaf with the rice, press and turn, so we now have the other side of the algae leaf in front of us, the rice is below. Spread a little mayonnaise lengthways on the algae leaf, add the surimi lengthways to the mayo, cut the cucumber and avocado into sticks and add. Brush with a little wasabi and finally put a little Lollo Rosso on top. Now roll the whole thing in with the help of the bamboo mat.

### Nigiris with tuna and shrimps

To do this, cut the tuna into bite-sized thin slices, free shrimp from their shell. Brush both with a little wasabi. Moisten the hands, take some rice and roll it oval in the back of the hand and then press it into a box shape. Place the fish on the rice.

95

The number of nigiris in relation to the makis depends on your preferences, if you prefer makis, just make more sushi rolls. Here, a roll can of course also become completely vegetarian, for example with only avocado or shiitake mushrooms or with your own taste also varied with vegetables and fish. Of course, you can also use other sea creatures for the Nigiris, such as salmon, octopus, mackerel, scallop, etc. Just think in advance when shopping to adjust the amount of sea ingredients to your requirements. And make sure you always buy fresh fish, the best thing to say is that you want to make sushi.

For serving, cut the rolls into approx. 6 to 8 pieces, take a sharp knife and moisten them slightly before each cut, so you have clean cuts and no rice sticking anywhere on the edges of the roll. Arrange the pieces with the nigiris on a plate. Serve the pickled ginger and soy sauce in separate bowls. Both nigiris and makis can be dipped in the soy sauce, which gives additional taste, and the wasabi paste can also be added. The ginger is used to neutralize the taste between two different sushi snacks, but some also simply eat it.

Have fun rolling and enjoy your meal!

# SUSHI MIX 2

## INGREDIENTS FOR 6 PORTIONS

- 4 nori sheets
- 2 cups of rice (sushi rice)
- 3 tbsp of rice vinegar
- 1 tbsp of sugar
- 1 teaspoon of salt
- 2 tbsp of wasabi paste or 2 tbsp. Wasabi powder, mixed with water
- 2 tbsp of mayonnaise
- 1 teaspoon of spice mix (togarashi)
- 100 g of salmon (sushi quality)
- 100 g of tuna (sushi quality)
- Surimi
- ½ cucumber, peeled, seeded
- Avocado, seeded, without skin
- 6 large shrimps, raw, without head
- 1 disc of ginger, very thin, grated
- Salt
- 1 tbsp of sesame oil

- 2 tbsp of sesame, black
- 2 tbsp of caviar (tobiko - fly fish caviar)
- 6 discs of pancakes (japanese omelet)
- 2 teaspoons of caviar (trout caviar)
- 1 tbsp of cress
- 2 tbsp of ginger (gari - sushi ginger) from the glass or homemade
- 20 ml of soy sauce

# PREPARATION

Total time approx. 45 minutes

1. Sushi means using leavened rice. Raw fish does not have to be part of it. First, the vinegar is warmed up and mixed well with the sugar and salt. This process should take place days in advance because the longer the mixture is at rest, the better it gets. 4 weeks would be optimal and the mixture does not have to be refrigerated. Once the rice is acidified, it only lasts about a day.

2. The rice is washed until only clear water flows out. Then let it drain in the sieve for 30 minutes. It will work perfectly in a rice cooker with a pinch of salt. If you don't have a cooker, you can read the exact instructions in the database under my recipe "Japanese rice".

3. When the rice is ready, put it in a baking dish (not made of metal) and distribute it well. It would be better to use a Japanese wooden mold that is specially designed for sushi rice. Then pour the vinegar mixture over the rice and work it into it with a wooden spatula. Do not stir, but prick and turn horizontally to distribute the vinegar well.

4. To prevent it from cooling completely, so that the rice doesn't stick too much, cover it with a slightly damp cloth. If the rice is needed, it should only be at room temperature so that the contents are not cooked.

5. At the latest now all ingredients should be portioned. Cut two cucumbers, a salmon and tuna strand about 0.5 cm thick and a length the width of the nori sheet. Stone the avocado, remove the peel and trim on strands of equal thickness. These must then be put together later.

6.  Take the prawns out of their shells, remove the intestines and insert a toothpick lengthways so that they stay perfectly in shape. Now cook gently in the sesame oil, mix in the ginger and lightly salt, add a little Togarashi, set aside to cool.

7.  For maki sushi, the nori sheet is cut in half and one, with the rough side up, is placed on the lower half of a sushi bast mat. Now spread the rice about 0.5 cm thick with wet hands and press it on, while 1 - 2 cm remain free on the nori sheet. In the middle you put a cucumber strand and next to it a tuna strand, which you spread thinly with wasabi.

8.  Now roll up the nori sheet using the bast mat, pressing everything together relatively firmly. If necessary, moisten the vacant area on the nori sheet and close the roll there. Unroll the raffia mat again.

9.  First halve the maki roll and then cut it into 6 parts. The knife for this must be of very good quality and should be rinsed with warm water after each cut. Use the other half of the nori sheet to make another roll with avocado and salmon.

# SUSHI MIX 3

## INGREDIENTS FOR 6 PORTIONS

- 1 kg of sushi rice
- 10 nori sheets
- 200 g of salmon, fresh
- 100 g of shrimp
- ½ cucumber, about length of nori sheets
- ½ avocado
- Carrot, about the length of the nori leaves
- Sesame
- Mirin
- Soy sauce
- Wasabi powder
- Ginger pickled
- 4 tbsp of sugar

Also: (for the japanese omelet)

- Egg
- 1 teaspoon of soy sauce
- 2 teaspoons of mirin
- Sugar

# PREPARATION

Total time approx. 3 hours

1. First cook the sushi rice according to the package description. Meanwhile, heat 12 tablespoons of mirin with the sugar in a saucepan until the sugar has dissolved. Then pour the Mirin-Sud onto the finished sushi rice and fold in. Let the rice cool down.

2. Cut the cucumber, carrots and avocado into thin strips, adapting them to the length of the nori sheets. Do the same with some of the salmon, cut the other half into wider, short but thin pieces, which are later added to the nigiri. Cut the shrimp either lengthways so that they are flat on the nigiris or leave them untrimmed.

3. Wrap the bamboo mat with cling film so that no rice sticks in between and put a nori sheet on top. I cut away a third of each nori sheet and use this smaller part for the inside-out rolls, so the maki have a nice size. When the rice has cooled, spread a layer of rice on one of the nori sheets and make sure that the layer is not too thick. Now place either strips of fish, cucumber, carrot or avocado at the beginning of the roll and roll the roll with light pressure using the sushi mat.Put sesame seeds on a larger plate. For the inside-out rolls, put rice directly on the mat covered with cling film. Place the smaller part of the norbi leaf on top and fill again with strips of vegetables or fish. Now roll with the mat and turn the finished roll in sesame.

4. Form small amounts of rice for the nigiri and top with the salmon and prawns. You can also top it with omelette. For the Japanese omelet, I whisked 2 eggs, 1 teaspoon of soy sauce and 2 teaspoons of mirin with a little sugar and let them stand in the pan over low heat. Then cut into thin, wide slices, which can then be placed on the nigiri. I cut thin strips from a nori sheet here, wrap them in the middle around the nigiri and moisten them a little with a mixture of water and mirin.

5. Cut the sushi rolls into bite-size pieces and arrange them on serving plates with the nigiri. Mix wasabi powder with water or use ready paste. Place the soy sauce in shallow bowls and arrange the pickled ginger.

# SUSHI BURRITO WITH TURKEY, MANGO AND AVOCADO

## INGREDIENTS FOR 2 PORTIONS

- 200 g of sushi rice
- 2 tbsp of rice vinegar
- Sugar
- 200 g of turkey breast
- Cucumber
- Mango, ripe
- Avocado, ripe
- Arugula
- 3 tbsp of peanuts, salted
- 100 g of crème fraiche cheese
- 100 g of cream cheese
- Lemons
- 2 tbsp of oil, neutral
- Chili flakes
- Salt and pepper
- 4 nori sheets
- Soy sauce

# PREPARATION

Total time approx. 1 hour 10 minutes

1.  So that the sushi rice has cooled down to roll, you should prepare it first. First wash the sushi rice thoroughly. Then prepare the rice according to the package instructions or simply in a rice cooker. Shouldn't take longer than 20-30 minutes.

2.  In the meantime, heat the rice vinegar in a small saucepan and stir with 1 tsp salt and 1 tsp sugar until the salt and sugar have dissolved. Place the finished sushi rice in a large bowl with the vinegar mixture and stir in well with a wooden spoon. Then set the sushi rice aside and let it cool.

3.  Now the filling can be prepared: Peel the mango, cucumber and avocado and cut into strips.Cut the turkey breast into fine strips and fry in a pan with a little oil, salting and peppering.

4.  Squeeze half a lemon for the cream. In a bowl, stir in the crème fraîche, cream cheese and 1 tablespoon of oil, add a little lemon juice, chili flakes, salt, pepper and sugar, depending on your taste, and mix. Chop peanuts and set aside in a bowl.

5.  Provide all ingredients - sushi rice, cucumber, mango, avocado, peanuts, cream and arugula, as well as the bamboo mats with one nori sheet each.

6.  Now it's time to fill and roll! To do this, dip your fingers in a bowl of water so that the rice does not stick to your fingers as much. Now distribute the sushi rice on the nori sheet. Cut out an inch. Spread a blob of the delicious cream in the middle of the seaweed sheet. Top with a few strips of turkey, cucumber, mango and avocado. Sprinkle with arugula and peanuts. Now drizzle the end of the algae leaf with water so that the nori leaf sticks to the end of the rolling when it is closed. Roll the sushi burrito from the bottom up. Press firmly on the roller. The finished sushi burrito can still be wrapped in baking paper or aluminum foil and cut in half diagonally. Place the soy sauce in a small bowl for dipping. Good Appetite!

# SUSHI BALLS

## INGREDIENTS FOR 1 PORTIONS

- 1 port of rice, sushi finished
- Wasabi paste
- 200 g of salmon, smoked, cut into pieces the size of postage stamps
- 1 point of shrimp
- 50 g of roe from the fly fish
- Pickled cucumber, thinly sliced
- 100 g of roast beef, cut into thin slices the size of postage stamps
- 100 g of tuna cut into pieces the size of postage stamps
- Radish, japanese, pickled, cut into postage-sized pieces

# PREPARATION

Total time approx. 30 minutes

1. Halve the amount of rice. Spread a piece of cling film about 10x10 cm in size on the work surface and place a piece of smoked salmon in the middle. Spread a little wasabi on the salmon. Form 1 tablespoon sushi rice into a loose ball and place on top.

2. Lift and twist all 4 corners of the cling film to compress fish and rice into a tight ball. Do the same with the cucumber slices.

3. For the shrimp balls, place a shrimp in the middle of the cling film and put some fly fry in the bend. Form another tablespoon of rice into a loose ball, put on the shrimp and form a firm ball with the foil.

4. The finished balls can be kept in the cling film until shortly before serving.

5. Arrange on a plate and serve with soy sauce and pickled ginger.

# CUCUMBER SUSHI

## INGREDIENTS FOR 2 PORTIONS

- Cucumber (one as straight as possible)
- 75 g of rice (sushi or milk rice)
- 2 tbsp of vinegar (rice vinegar)
- ½ tsp of salt
- Wasabi paste or horseradish
- 100 g of smoked salmon
- 15 g of caviar
- Cress
- Sugar
- 200 ml of water, salted

# PREPARATION

Total time approx. 30 minutes

1. Wash the rice cold repeatedly until the water remains as clear as possible. Then bring to the boil once in 150 ml - 200 ml of salt water, then cook in a low heat with the lid closed in about 10-15 minutes.

2. Season the warm rice with rice vinegar, salt and sugar and let it cool. For warm sushi, use the rice immediately without letting it cool down.

3. Wash and peel the cucumber. Halve lengthways and scrape out the core with a teaspoon. Brush the inside of the cucumber with wasabi paste or horseradish, then pour the rice into the cucumber halves. Cut everything into 2-3 cm diamonds. Put a little smoked salmon or a pinch of caviar on each piece and serve garnished with cress.

# DITHMARSCHER SUSHI

## INGREDIENTS FOR 6 PORTIONS

- Radish
- Kohlrabi
- Apple
- Pear
- ½ mackerel, smoked
- ¼ eel, (smoked eel)
- Matjes filet
- 12 shrimp, smoked

# PREPARATION

Total time approx. 25 minutes

1. This recipe was quasi "obeying the need" in Dithmarschen and was extremely well received.

2. The ingredients are completely variable, you can use any solid smoked fish, but also smoked salmon or, for example, a mixture of crabs, mackerel whip and a dash of lemon. You can also vary vegetables or fruit, of course it must be a vegetable that can be eaten raw.

3. Preparation: Cut equal sized pieces of 2cm x 4cm from the fruit and / or vegetables.

4. Also cut different types of fish or seafood (by the way, the slightly salty matjes tastes great, for example, on canned pears!) Into pieces of the same size that fit on the vegetable pieces.

5. Now arrange the parts on a plate and use toothpicks instead of chopsticks for pricking.

# OSHI SUSHI

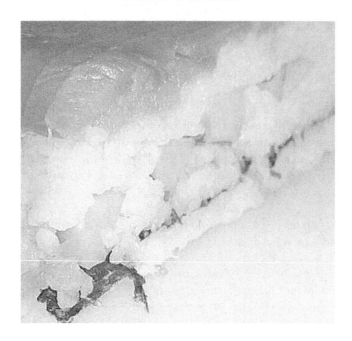

## INGREDIENTS FOR 8 PORTIONS

- 400 g of rice (sushi rice), ready prepared (see basic recipe)
- ¼ salad cucumber, cut lengthways
- 8 king prawns without head with shell
- 4 tbsp of sake
- 1 teaspoon of wasabi paste
- Salt

# PREPARATION

Total time approx. 20 minutes

1.  Line a baking tin with cling film.

2.  Wash the shrimps, dry them, and fix them lengthways with a roulade needle. Bring some salted water to the boil with the sake in a saucepan. Switch off the hotplate and let the shrimp soak in the broth until they turn red. Peel and halve the shrimp and remove the intestine.

3.  Wash the cucumber and halve lengthways. Remove the seeds and pat the cucumber halves dry. 5 Cut approximately 0.5 cm wide strips that are as long as the shape. Sprinkle the cucumber with a little sea salt, let it steep for approx. 30 min and pat dry again.

4.  Brush the shrimp on the white inside with a little wasabi paste and place them side by side on the bottom of the mold so that the red outer skin comes to rest on the transparent film, cover with half of the sushi rice. Place the cucumber strips on the rice, press down lightly and cover with the rest of the rice. Fold the cling film over the rice so that everything is covered. With a second mold, a lid or the like. Cover, press gently and weigh down evenly with a weight so that the Oshi sushi is pressed evenly and firmly.

5.  After 30-40 minutes, throw the Oshi Sushi out of the mold onto a board. Carefully remove the cling film and cut the Oshi Sushi into 8 parts with a sharp knife.

# SUSHI SANDWICH

## INGREDIENTS FOR 1 PORTIONS

- 100 g of tofu
- Soy sauce
- 1 teaspoon of chili flakes
- Ginger
- Garlic cloves
- 2 nori sheets
- 70 g of sushi rice
- 30 g of avocado
- 6 g of baby spinach
- 50 g of red cabbage
- 30 ml of rice vinegar
- 5 ml of maple syrup
- Sea-salt
- ½ garlic cloves

# PREPARATION

Total time approx. 1 hour 25 minutes

1.  Marinate the tofu with the soy sauce, the clove of garlic, 1 teaspoon chili flakes and a little chopped ginger. Meanwhile cook the sushi rice according to the package instructions. Fry the marinated tofu in a non-stick pan for about 3 minutes on all sides.

2.  Peel the avocado, remove the core and cut into slices. Wash the baby spinach and pat dry with kitchen paper.

3.  For the red cabbage salad, wash 30 g of red cabbage and cut into narrow strips. Put the rice vinegar, maple syrup, a little sea salt and ½ clove of garlic with a little water in a saucepan and bring to a boil over medium heat. Pour the warm dressing over the red cabbage, mix well, cool and let it soak.

4.  Use a small bowl to bring the sushi rice into a square shape, place it in the middle of the nori sheet and place the baby spinach leaves on it. Now press a little red cabbage salad onto the spinach with a fork and spread a few slices of the avocado on top. Finally cut the marinated tofu in half lengthways, cut smaller if necessary and place on the avocado slices. When arranging all ingredients, make sure that they are placed as close together as possible and layered in the shape of a square. Now moisten the fingertips with a little water and glue the corners of the sheet together in the middle of the sandwich so that the ingredients are well wrapped in the nori sheet. Moisten again with water if a corner of the sheet should not stick immediately.

5.  Halve the sandwich and serve with soy sauce.

# VEGGIE ONIGIRI

## INGREDIENTS FOR 12 PORTIONS

- 250 g of sushi rice
- ½ tsp of salt
- 1 teaspoon of sugar
- 1 shot of sake
- 1 smaller broccoli
- 1 handful corn
- 1 handful gouda, grated
- 1 cup of cream cheese
- Cucumber
- Avocado
- 1 nori sheet

# PREPARATION

Total time approx. 1 hour 40 minutes

1. Cook the sushi rice according to the instructions, e.g. Bring to the boil, cook for 10 minutes on a low flame, remove from the stove for 10 minutes and let cook.

2. While the sushi is cooking rice, prepare the broccoli so that it has time to cool down. Peel the avocado and cut it into small pieces. Peel the cucumber and cut it into small cubes.

3. Place the salt, sugar and sake in a cold bowl (metal, unpainted wood or stone) and mix, then add the sushi rice.

4. Let the sushi rice cool, e.g. Put the rice in a bowl in cold water or in the refrigerator and best stir again and again, then it cools down faster.

5. Press a teaspoon-sized mass of the cooled sushi rice flat in your hand, then add any cold ingredients: - a level teaspoon of cream cheese and three small pieces of avocado

6. Some cream cheese with a few cubes of cucumber. Some corn with Gouda, a few florets with broccoli and some cream cheese.

7. Then flatten a small amount of rice in the other hand and place it on top to seal the onigiri.

8. Both the corn and the broccoli filling are a bit of a mess, so it's best not to seal the onigiri but to mix the sushi rice with the filling in hand.

9. The cucumber and the Philadelphia should also be mixed in a bowl, this makes preparation easier.

10. Press the onigiri into small shapes (traditionally triangular) and press an approximately thumb-sized piece of nori sheet to one side. This is mainly intended not to get your fingers dirty when consumed.

# ONIGIRI WITH SALMON AND CHICKEN

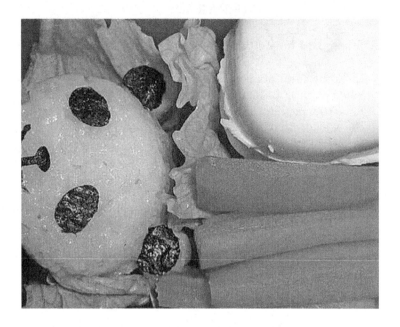

## INGREDIENTS FOR 2 PORTIONS

- 2 cups of rice (short grain rice)
- 100 g of salmon, smoked, or very fresh
- 100 g of chicken breast fillet
- 4 nori sheets
- 3 tbsp of vinegar (sushi-zu), ready-made sushi vinegar for seasoning the rice
- Wasabi paste
- Soy sauce, for dipping
- Mayonnaise
- Spice mix (furikake)

# PREPARATION

Total time approx. 30 minutes

1. Rinse the short grain rice in a sieve until the water remains clear. Place in a saucepan with 4 cups of water. Bring rice to a boil over high heat. As soon as foam in the pot threatens to rise, turn off the stove and let the rice rest on the warm stove for 15 minutes. Very important: While the rice is boiling and then resting, never remove the lid. Determining when the rice is cooking is best done with a glass-lid pot.

2. Season the still hot rice with the sushi and let it cool.

3. In the meantime, dice the chicken breast fillet, season and fry. Dice the salmon. Cut each nori sheet into 5 strips of equal size.

4. Now form balls out of the rice. The easiest way is with an onigiri shape, which comes in different shapes and sizes. Fill rice balls in the middle with salmon or chicken. Add a swab of mayonnaise to fill as you like.

5. Brush the finished onigiri with a little wasabi paste and wrap each with a strip of nori.

# TOAST SUSHI ROLLS

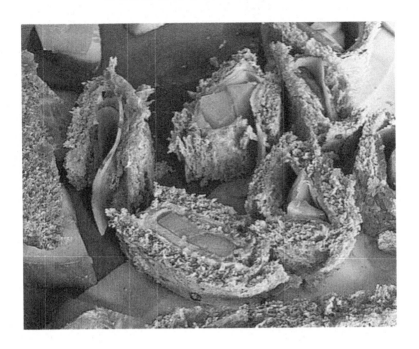

## INGREDIENTS FOR 1 PORTIONS

- 500 g of toasted bread (whole grain)
- 200 g of cream cheese
- Milk
- Salt
- Pepper
- 1 cucumber
- 1 carrot
- 1 salami

# PREPARATION

Total time approx. 20 minutes

1.  Debark the toasted bread, then roll it out very flat with the rolling pin. Whip cream cheese with 1-2 tablespoons of milk and season with salt and pepper.

2.  Cut the other ingredients into pens about 1-2 cm thick. The length of the pens depends on the toasted bread - they should be a little longer than this is wide. Spread the cream cheese thinly on the toast slices and top with a cucumber, carrot and salami stick. Then roll up as tight as possible - the best way to do this is with a sushi mat. Cut sushi of approx. 4 cm each with a very sharp knife with a smooth cutting edge.

3.  Filling variations:
    -   Only cucumber, only carrot or only avocado
    -   smoked salmon
    -   Egg and herb spread (instead of cream cheese) and cooked ham
    -   Bell pepper - Cream cheese without salt and pepper and jam, such as strawberry, raspberry etc.

# TOAST ROLLS WITH SALMON CREAM CHEESE FILLING

## INGREDIENTS FOR 1 PORTIONS

- 6 discs of toasted bread, whole grain
- 150 g of cream cheese
- 200 g of smoked salmon
- Pepper
- Dill
- Horseradish, optional

## PREPARATION

Total time approx. 1 hour 20 minutes

1. First cut the rind off the toast slices, then roll the toast slices flat with a pasta roll (alternatively glass bottle). Spread the cream cheese thinly on the toast slices and top them with smoked salmon. Season to taste and add horseradish if necessary.
2. Roll up the toast slices, then wrap in aluminum or plastic wrap. Then place the rolls in the refrigerator for at least 1 hour so that the toast becomes softer and easier to cut. For serving, they are cut into 6 to 8 pieces (just like sushi).

# DISHES

# TUNA TARTARE ON AVOCADO CREAM

## INGREDIENTS FOR 2 PORTIONS

For the fish:

- 250 g of tuna, frozen or sushi quality
- Shallot
- ¼ cucumber
- Oil
- Salt and pepper

For the salad:

- 50 g of lamb's lettuce
- Pomegranate

For the dip:

- Avocado, ripe
- Lemon juice
- Salt

Also: (for the parmesan crackers)

- 50 g of parmesan
- Salt and pepper

Furthermore:

- Horseradish
- Wasabi paste
- Some stems of cress

# PREPARATION

Total time approx. 1 hour 3 minutes

1. Cut the tuna very small, as well as the shallots and the cucumber. Mix the three ingredients together, season with salt, pepper and a little neutral oil and stir well.

2. Chop the parmesan finely, add a little salt and pepper and spread it on a baking sheet lined with baking paper. Bake in the oven at 200 ° C for approx. 8 minutes until the cheese has combined and is golden yellow. Let the cheese cool and set aside. This can also be prepared very well hours in advance.

3. Wash the lamb's lettuce well and "pulp" the seeds from the pomegranate.

4. Puree the avocado with a blender and add a little lemon juice and salt.

5. Now arrange the avocado cream on the plate and the tuna mixture using a serving ring, fill up the cream. Arrange the lamb's lettuce with the pomegranate seeds, decorate a dollop of horseradish and wasabi, garnish the whole thing with cress and add a little of the Parmesan pieces.

6. It goes with fresh baguette.

# SPICY TUNA TARTARE

## INGREDIENTS FOR 4 PORTIONS

- 2 tsp of heaped ginger, fresh, finely chopped or grated
- 100 ml of vegetable oil
- 400 g of tuna, sushi quality
- 2 tbsp of coriander green, finely chopped
- Chili pepper, seeded and finely chopped
- 1 tbsp of spring onion, finely chopped
- 3 tsp of lime juice
- Sea-salt
- Pepper
- 1 tomato, peeled and seeded

# PREPARATION

Total time approx. 1 day 20 minutes

1.  Soak the ginger in oil the day before and leave in the fridge. Cut the tuna into small cubes and place in a cold bowl.

2.  Mix the chopped chili pepper, the spring onion, 3 teaspoons of lime juice and 4 teaspoons of the ginger oil with the pieces of ginger with a tablespoon of coriander. Salt and pepper.

3.  Place in the middle of the plates using serving rings. Drizzle the remaining ginger oil around the tartare, put the finely chopped tomato pieces on top, then the rest of the coriander. Drizzle with lime juice.

# TUNA TARTARE WITH CORIANDER PESTO

## INGREDIENTS FOR 4 PORTIONS

- 1 bunch coriander
- 50 g of parmesan
- Olive oil
- 2 toes of garlic
- ½ tsp of salt
- 1 shot of gin, dry or wormwood
- 1 tbsp of lemon juice or lime juice
- Soy sauce
- 150 g of tuna, fresher

# PREPARATION

Total time approx. 20 minutes

1. Scrape the fresh tuna off the whole piece with a normal tablespoon so that you get a coarse tartare. Mix this well with lemon juice, a little olive oil, gin and 1 - 1.5 tablespoons of soy sauce and, ideally, keep cool and covered.

2. Roughly chop the coriander and garlic for the pesto. If the parmesan is not grated, grate it. Fill with the pine nuts and salt in a tall container and chop with a hand blender. Fill up with olive oil until a mass with the consistency of toothpaste is created. Mix these in a ratio of 1: 3 from pesto to tartare with the tuna tartare and season with soy sauce.

3. As a variation, you can also replace about a quarter of the coriander with Thai basil or refine the tartare with some finely chopped ginger.

4. The rest of the pesto is kept in a closed container in the refrigerator for at least a week and goes well with pasta or starters.

# REFINED TUNA TARTARE

## INGREDIENTS FOR 6 PORTIONS

- 500 g of tuna, sushi-quality fillets
- 3 m of tomatoes
- Snake cucumber
- 3 tbsp of soy sauce
- 1 tsp of chili powder, red
- 1 bunch of coriander
- 1 splash of lemon juice
- 3 tbsp of olive oil, virgin
- 6 discs of pumpernickel
- 100 g of cream cheese e.g. Philadelphia

# PREPARATION

Total time approx. 4 hours

1. Wash the tuna fillet, pat dry and place in the freezer for 5 hours. Cut this fillet, which is not completely frozen, with a very sharp knife into very thin slices (2 - 3 mm) and then process these slices into very small cubes using longitudinal and cross-sections. Due to the frozen condition, the fish can be worked very well with a knife.

2. Slice the tomatoes in a cross shape and place in boiling water for 1 - 2 minutes, then skin and quarter. Lift out the core casing with a large tablespoon and cut the tomato meat into small cubes (similar size to the tuna fillet).

3. Process the cucumber with a peeler and cut into two lengthways. Here too, scrape out the core casing with a large tablespoon and then cut the cucumber meat into small cubes similar to the tomatoes and fillet.

4. Clean the bunch of coriander under running water, shake off the water and shred with a 4 or 5-blade herb scissors. Put everything that has been chopped up so far with the remaining ingredients in a large mixing bowl and mix at low speed with a hand mixer with a dough hook.

5. Put the tartare in a container and let it steep in the refrigerator for 2-3 hours.

6. Just take it out of the fridge just before serving, put everything in a large sieve, press something from the top with a cellar or similar so that the resulting free liquid can drain off. On large flat plates with serving rings, cut round slices out of the pumpernickel slices and fill the tartare in portions in the rings, press on a little with a very thin layer of cream cheese and decorate with a sheet of coriander. Lift off the serving rings and decorate the plate with a few drops of soy sauce.

# SALMON TARTARE WITH LEMON CREAM

## INGREDIENTS FOR 4 PORTIONS

- 400 g of salmon fillet, sushi quality
- 200 g of smoked salmon
- 1 bar of leek
- Garlic
- 1½ tsp of honey
- 2 tbsp of olive oil
- 150 g of crème fraiche cheese
- 4 tsp of caviar (salmon)
- Cress
- Lemon, organic
- Salt and pepper

# PREPARATION

Total time approx. 20 minutes

1. Finely dice the two types of salmon and finely dice the garlic.

2. Cut the leek in half into very thin half rings.

3. Mix everything with a marinade made from honey, olive oil and half the juice of the lemon and the grated lemon peel. Season with salt and pepper if desired. Season the crème fraiche with the remaining lemon juice and salt and pepper.

4. Arrange the tartare in metal rings or large biscuit cutters, spread the lemon cream on top. Garnish with cress. A little fresh baguette may also be enough.

# TUNA CARPACCIO

## INGREDIENTS FOR 4 PORTIONS

- 125 ml of oil
- 60 ml of lime juice
- 2 tbsp of fish sauce
- ¼ tsp of pepper, black, freshly ground
- Sugar
- 400 g of tuna, sushi - quality
- 3 tbsp of coriander green, roughly chopped

## PREPARATION

Total time approx. 15 minutes

1. Cut the tuna into very fine slices, freeze if necessary beforehand. Prepare the dressing, pour half on a plate. Place the tuna slices on top of each other and cover with the rest of the dressing.
2. Marinate in the refrigerator for at least 30 minutes.
3. Sprinkle with coriander before serving.

# HAND CHEESE

## INGREDIENTS FOR 4 PORTIONS

- 200 g of cheese (hand cheese) without caraway
- Shallot, chopped
- 2 tbsp of vinegar (sushi vinegar)
- 2 tbsp of cider
- 1 tbsp of peanut oil
- 1 teaspoon of peppercorns (cubeb pepper)
- ¼ tsp of cayenne pepper
- 1 pinch of salt and pepper, black from the mill

## PREPARATION

Total time approx. 30 minutes

1. Cut the hand cheese into slices and place in a bowl. Sprinkle the chopped shallots over it.
2. Mix the remaining ingredients into a marinade and bring to the boil briefly. Pour hot over the hand cheese. Let cool for 20 minutes.
3. Spread on plates and serve sprinkled with black pepper.

# PANGASIUS ON FENNEL SALAD IN ORANGE VINAIGRETTE

## INGREDIENTS FOR 4 PORTIONS

- 500 g of fish fillet (pangasius fillet), ready to cook
- 1 toe of garlic
- 1 branch of thyme
- Oil, for frying
- 2 tuber fennels
- Orange, organic
- 3 tbsp of vinegar, (sushi vinegar)
- 1 tbsp of oil, (orange oil)
- 5 tbsp of olive oil
- Salt
- Pepper

# PREPARATION

Total time approx. 30 minutes

1.  If necessary, finely grate the orange peel or tear the zests and mix with the olive oil to produce an "orange oil".

2.  Peel the oranges, remove the fillets with a small knife and set aside. Squeeze the juice of the remaining orange and collect in a bowl. First add vinegar, salt, sugar and pepper while stirring until the spices have dissolved. Now slowly add the oils (orange oil and olive oil) and stir into a dressing.

3.  Set fennel green aside for decoration. Clean fennel and cut into thin slices, better plan. Put in the bowl and marinate with the dressing. Add the orange fillets.

4.  If necessary, portion the fish. Fry and cook briefly on both sides in a pan with the oil, the pressed garlic and the thyme. Season with salt and pepper.

5.  Serving: First arrange the fennel salad with the orange fillets on a plate. Place the fish on top and decorate with fennel green. Good Appetite!

# MARINATED TUNA ON A NORI AND RICE BED

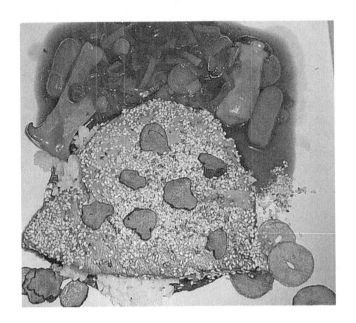

## INGREDIENTS FOR 2 PORTIONS

- Tuna fillet
- 4 nori sheets
- 2 bars of leek
- 3 bars of spring onions
- Carrot
- 4 tbsp of sesame
- 3 toes of garlic
- 10 tbsp of soy sauce
- 6 tbsp of sake
- ½ tsp of sambal oelek
- 2 teaspoons of wasabi paste
- 1 tbsp of sugar
- 125 g of rice, sushi
- 2 tbsp of rice vinegar
- Oil, (peanut oil)

# PREPARATION

Total time approx. 1 hour 20 minutes

1. Mix the soy sauce, sake and sugar in a bowl until the sugar has completely dissolved. Then marinate the tuna fillets (preferably sushi quality) in a closed bowl for at least 30 minutes. In the meantime, clean the vegetables and cut them into small slices.

2. Roast sesame seeds in a pan (without adding fat) while stirring constantly until they turn brown. Then take out and set aside.

3. Remove the tuna fillets from the marinade and set aside. Place the marinade in a wok (or a suitable pan) and add the wasabi paste and sambal oelek. Heat the liquid on a low setting and add the vegetables (except the garlic). Let it simmer for about 20 minutes.

4. Cook the sushi rice for 15 minutes according to the instructions, drain, add rice vinegar and leave covered for another 15 minutes.

5. Fry the tuna fillets in peanut oil on both sides for about 90 seconds and then turn both sides in the sesame seeds. Then add the garlic to the oil and roast while stirring. Do not let it burn!

6. Divide the nori sheet and place one half on each plate. Then moisten slightly. Place the rice in the middle of the nori sheet and distribute it about the size of the tuna fillet.

7. Place the tuna on the rice bed, put the garlic on the tuna and spread vegetables with liquid around the rice bed.

# ASIAN COLESLAW WITH GLAZED SALMON FILLET

## INGREDIENTS FOR 4 PORTIONS

- 800 g of white cabbage
- 1 tbsp of salt
- 2 tbsp of sugar
- Lemon, the juice of it
- 200 g of carrot
- 6 stems mint
- Sesame oil, toasted
- 25 g of ginger, (sushi ginger) pickled
- 2 teaspoons of soy sauce
- 3 tbsp of honey
- Chili sauce, (thai sweet chili sauce)
- Salmon fillet
- Oil, for frying

# PREPARATION

Total time approx. 30 minutes

1. Roughly grate the white cabbage. Mix with salt and sugar and knead vigorously with your hands. Squeeze out the lemon juice and add it. Peel the carrots and grate them roughly. Wash the mint, dry it, pluck the leaves and cut them finely. Mix everything with the herb and season with the sesame oil.

2. Finely chop the ginger and mix with soy sauce, honey and the chilli sauce. Heat the oil in a pan and fry the salmon until crispy on both sides. Turn off the stove and spread the sauce over the salmon. Turn several times and let glaze briefly.

3. Arrange salmon with the coleslaw.

# SIMPLE POKE BOWL

## INGREDIENTS FOR 2 PORTIONS

- 1 cup of jasmine rice
- 300 g of salmon (sushi salmon) or smoked salmon
- 1 small can of pineapple
- 50 g of algae, steamed
- 1 small cucumber
- Bell pepper, red
- Tomatoes
- Avocado
- 1 tbsp of sesame
- 2 tbsp of soy sauce
- 4 tbsp of sesame oil
- 1 small piece of ginger

# PREPARATION

Total time approx. 20 minutes

1.  The Poke bowl is a mixture of sushi and Buddha bowl, can be varied to your heart's content and refrigerator contents and is super healthy!

2.  Simply cook the rice according to the package instructions, let it cool a little and spread it over 2 bowls. Then arrange the finely chopped vegetables on top. Prepare a dressing from sesame oil, soy sauce and grated ginger and pour over it. Sprinkle with sesame seeds and serve.

# TAMAGOYAKI SUSHI OMELETTE

## INGREDIENTS FOR 2 PORTIONS

- 6 eggs
- 50 ml of dashi
- Water
- 1 tbsp of sake
- 1 teaspoon of mirin
- 1 tbsp of soy sauce, good quality
- 20 g of sugar
- 1 pinch of salt
- 2 tbsp of oil

# PREPARATION

Total time approx. 30 minutes

1.  Bring the dashi, sake, mirin and sugar to the boil for 1 minute so that everything mixes better and the alcohol evaporates, then let it cool. Beat the eggs with a little salt and the soy sauce until they are foamy, then mix the dashi mass, which has cooled down, with it.

2.  Now you need a rectangular, Japanese pan, but you can also try to prepare a Japanese omelet in round pans. You could later cut everything into a large rectangle and use the trimmed edges for something else.

3.  Spread a little oil in the pan and add about 1/4 of the egg mass. If it sticks to the floor, beat a quarter of the area from the outside in, folding it like a piece of paper for a letter. Then fold the 2nd and 3rd quarters over the next one. Now spread some oil on the free bottom of the pan again and fill thinly with egg mass. Fold them, starting with the egg mass already folded, in the same way as before. Repeat these two steps two more times until the egg mass is used up. This creates a relatively increased role. Let the roll slide on a board, degrease with kitchen paper on the outside and cut into even slices of approx. 1-2 cm.

4.  Either eat immediately or use at room temperature for nigiri sushi. The omelet tastes pure when cooled.

# INARI SUSHI

## INGREDIENTS FOR 4 PORTIONS

- 220 g of rice, sushi
- 500 ml of water
- 2 tbsp of sesame, japanese, white
- 2 tbsp of rice vinegar
- 1 tbsp of sugar
- 1 tbsp of mirin
- 1 teaspoon of salt
- 12 tofu bags (inari bags)

# PREPARATION

Total time approx. 1 hour 40 minutes

1. Wash rice in a colander under running water, drain well. Bring water and rice to a boil. Reduce the heat and simmer for 4-5 minutes without the lid until the water is absorbed. Put the lid on and let stand for a further 4-5 minutes on low heat, then remove from the heat and let it swell in the closed pot for 10 minutes.

2. Roast the sesame seeds in a dry pan until golden brown for 3-4 minutes and gently swirl them in between; then take it out immediately.

3. Mix the vinegar, sugar, mirin and salt and add to the rice. Stir with a wooden spoon until the rice has cooled.

4. Carefully detach and open the Inari bags. Fill each with 1 tablespoon of rice. Sprinkle the rice with toasted sesame seeds, then squeeze the bag closed. Arrange on a platter and serve.

NOTE:

- Inari bags are stuffed bags made from deep fried tofu. You can buy them in Asian grocery stores.

# SUSHI PATTIES

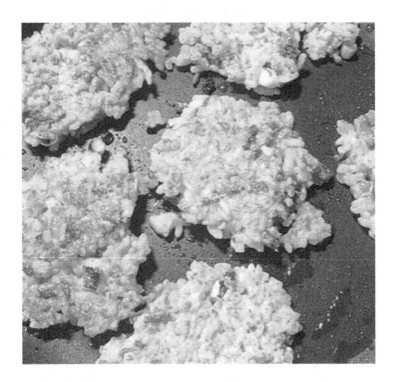

## INGREDIENTS FOR 2 PORTIONS

- 2 cups of rice, (normal long grain rice) or at will
- 2 cups of millet, (golden millet)
- 4 nori sheets
- 1 teaspoon of broth, instant (without yeast)
- Egg
- 1 teaspoon of flour
- Soy sauce
- Olive oil, or sesame oil
- Water
- Breadcrumbs

# PREPARATION

Total time approx. 1 hour

1. Place 2 espresso cups full of rice and millet in a saucepan, fill with 3 espresso cups of water and add a teaspoon of broth powder, let simmer for 10 minutes (with the lid on), then set the hob down and let it swell again on the hob for 15 minutes.

2. Cut the nori sheet into fine strips (best with scissors) and add to the rice and millet mixture with the egg and a teaspoon of flour (to bind), mix well. If the mass is too liquid (it should be a firm paste), you can add some breadcrumbs. Those who do not suffer from HI can still season with a little soy sauce, otherwise add a little salt (try the mass beforehand).

3. Heat some sesame oil in a pan (please use olive oil for HI) (medium heat) and add 4-5 piles into the pan with the help of 2 tablespoons, press a little flat, fry on both sides until golden brown.

4. It goes very well with (very un-Asian) cucumber salad.

5. If you like, you can of course play with other spices, but the nori leaves have their own taste that you shouldn't "kill" with spices that are too strong.

# VEGAN GOLUBTSI ON BRAISED VEGETABLES

## INGREDIENTS FOR 1 PORTIONS

For the parcels:

- 8 sheets of white cabbage
- 70 g of sushi rice
- 40 g of sliced (pea cutlet), alternatively soybean cutlet, fine
- 1 teaspoon of vegetable broth powder
- ½ tsp of smoked salt
- ½ tsp of pepper
- Bay leaf
- 1 small pickles

For the vegetables:

- ½ onion
- Leek stick
- 1 small carrot
- ½ smaller celery

- ½ pepper
- 2 m in size tomatoes
- 1 teaspoon of vegetable broth powder
- ½ tsp of salt
- ½ tsp of pepper
- 1 teaspoon of paprika powder
- Cornstarch
- 1 tbsp of oil for frying

# PREPARATION

Total time approx. 2 hours

1. Blanch the white cabbage leaves in salted water until the leaves are soft and slightly transparent. Drain the white cabbage leaves and let them cool.

2. Simmer the sushi rice with the vegetable stock powder, salt, pepper and the bay leaf in sufficient water according to the package for approx. 10 minutes. Stir occasionally and add the pea cutlet. Dice the pickled cucumber and add to the rice mince mixture. Let the pea cutlet go with the rice for a few minutes. The liquid should be completely absorbed. Now let the mixture cool and remove the bay leaf.

3. While the mass cools, wash, clean and cut the vegetables into small cubes. Put the oil in a saucepan or roaster, fry the vegetables in it until it has some color and season with the specified spices. Then add water to the vegetables until almost covered and simmer.

4. In the meantime, put the rice-chop mixture on the cabbage leaves, roll once, fold in the sides and continue rolling up. Place the golubtsi on the vegetables with the open side down. Let the cabbage rolls simmer on a low setting for about 45 minutes with the lid closed. At the end of the cooking time, tie the vegetables with a little cornstarch.

# SUSHI BOWL

## INGREDIENTS FOR 4 PORTIONS

- 500 g of sushi rice
- 50 ml of rice wine
- 4 avocados
- Cucumber
- 1 can of ginger, pickled, approx.100g
- 250 g of salmon, smoked or cooked
- 150 g of shrimp, cooked
- 4 nori sheets
- Handful sesame
- Soy sauce
- Mayonnaise
- Sriracha sauce

# PREPARATION

Total time approx. 2 hours 40 minutes

1.  Cook the sushi rice with rice wine according to the package instructions, then let it cool and chill.

2.  Cut avocados, cucumber, salmon, shrimp and nori leaves into small pieces.

3.  Drizzle the rice with soy sauce and garnish with all the ingredients.

4.  Mix a new sauce from mayonnaise and sriracha sauce and stain all ingredients with it.

# JAPANESE SEAWEED SALAD

## INGREDIENTS FOR 4 PORTIONS

- 1 bag of wakame, dried seaweed (in a bag are 56 grams)
- 3 tbsp of vinegar, (sushi, rice)
- 3 tbsp of sesame oil
- 1 tbsp of lime juice
- 1 tbsp of ginger, freshly grated
- 1 tbsp of sugar
- 1 toe of garlic, pressed
- 2 tbsp of coriander green, finely chopped
- ½ tbsp of chili powder
- 1 tbsp of sesame

# PREPARATION

Total time approx. 1 hour 20 minutes

1.  Pour seaweed on with hot water and leave for 10 min. to let go.

2.  Prepare the sauce:

3.  Mix all of the above ingredients (except the seaweed and sesame seeds) in a small bowl until smooth. Season with the chili powder depending on the hotness.

4.  Drain the seaweed and wring it out a little. Now simply fold the drained kelp under the sauce and sprinkle sesame seeds over it as you like. Let it brew for approx. 1 hour, preferably in the refrigerator.

# SUSHI SALAD

## INGREDIENTS FOR 2 PORTIONS

- 100 g of sushi rice, drier
- 150 ml of water
- 25 ml of rice vinegar
- 1 tbsp of sugar
- Salt
- 120 g of shrimp, pre-cooked
- 100 g of salmon, raw, fresh or frozen
- Cucumber
- 4 nori leaves (roasted seaweed)
- 1 tbsp of ginger, pickled, drained
- Lime
- ½ tsp of wasabi paste
- 1 tbsp of soy sauce
- 1 tbsp of sweet chili sauce

# PREPARATION

Total time approx. 1 hour 15 minutes

1. Wash the rice and gently simmer in a saucepan covered with water for 15 minutes (if necessary, add water), remove from the heat and let it swell again for 30 minutes.

2. Mix rice vinegar, 1 teaspoon sugar and 1/4 teaspoon salt and mix into the rice.

3. Peel, core and cut the cucumber into small cubes. Cut the nori sheets into small pieces (it works best with kitchen scissors). Also cut the salmon into small pieces. Then carefully mix everything - including the shrimp and ginger - with the cooled rice.

4. Squeeze the limes. Mix the wasabi, lime juice, soy sauce and sweet chili sauce and the remaining sugar and mix this dressing with the salad. Chill again and let it go through.

5. Do not store the salad for long as there is raw salmon in it.

# JAPANESE ONION SAUCE WITH CABBAGE AND SHRIMP

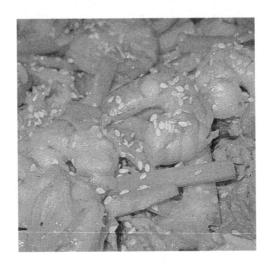

## INGREDIENTS FOR 2 PORTIONS

For the sauce:

- 1 m of onion
- 2 garlic cloves
- 2 tbsp of honey
- 4 tbsp of soy sauce, light
- 4 tbsp of sherry, dry
- 1 tbsp of tabasco or red pepper sauce
- 6 tbsp of sesame oil
- 2 tbsp of oyster sauce

For the salad:

- 1 smaller chinese cabbage
- Carrot
- ¼ cucumber
- 100 g of shrimp, cooked
- Sesame

# PREPARATION

Total time approx. 15 minutes

1.  For the sauce, roughly chop the onion, peel and quarter the garlic. Put in a blender with all ingredients and puree to a smooth sauce.

2.  Cut the Chinese cabbage into small pieces, remove the hard pieces and the stalk, blanch in salted water for 5 minutes, drain, quench with ice-cold water and let cool. Peel and cut the carrot so that you can cut 3 - 4 cm long thin sticks. Halve the cucumber, remove the seeds and also cut into 3 - 4 cm long thin sticks. Mix the cooled Chinese cabbage with about ¾ of the sauce and fill in small bowls. Decorate with carrot, cucumber sticks and shrimp, pour the remaining sauce over it and sprinkle with sesame seeds.

3.  Anyone who likes to eat sushi should have stumbled across a salad made with such a sauce. What exactly you take for a salad is of course a matter of taste, alternatives to Chinese cabbage would be iceberg or romaine lettuce, carrots and cucumber always look good in it and sesame is actually a must.

# PASTA SALAD WITH ROASTED BROCCOLI AND PEANUT-SILK TOFU SAUCE

## INGREDIENTS FOR 6 PORTIONS

- 80 ml of soy sauce, sweet (kikkoman sushi & sashimi)
- 150 ml of vegetable broth
- 100 g of tofu (silk tofu)
- 1 teaspoon of tabasco
- Garlic cloves
- 100 g of peanuts, roasted, salted
- 250 g of broccoli
- 4 tbsp of sesame oil
- 150 g of salad (lettuce hearts)
- 200 g of pasta (spaghetti), vegan
- Salt water
- 1 teaspoon of sesame oil
- 3 tbsp of roasted onions
- Salt
- Coriander green (4 - 6 stems)

# PREPARATION

Total time approx. 30 minutes

1. For the peanut sauce, puree the broth, the silk tofu, the chili sauce, the peeled garlic and 50 g peanuts (no more!) With a blender or a blender and add a little salt if necessary. The flavor of the broth and soy sauce is enough for my taste.

2. Cut the broccoli into thin slices, salt and fry in a wok or large pan in hot oil over medium heat for about 5 minutes. Meanwhile, cut the lettuce hearts into fine strips.

3. Cook the pasta in salted water according to the package instructions, cool under cold water and mix in a sieve with the sesame oil. If you want to eat it warm, leave out the step with the cold water!

4. Roughly chop the remaining 50 g of peanuts, then mix all the ingredients with the peanut sauce. Finally sprinkle the whole thing with the fried onions and serve (if you like) with plucked coriander leaves.

# SUSHI BOWL WITH TAMAGOYAKI

## INGREDIENTS FOR 2 PORTIONS

- 150 g of round grain rice
- ½ cucumber
- Bell pepper, red
- Carrot
- Avocado
- 2 tbsp of sesame
- 5 tbsp of rice vinegar
- 2 tbsp of sesame oil
- 2 tbsp of soy sauce
- Ginger powder
- Egg
- 3 tbsp of sake
- 1 teaspoon of soy sauce
- 2 teaspoons of sugar
- Salt

# PREPARATION

Total time approx. 45 minutes

1.  Prepare the rice according to the package instructions. Meanwhile wash the vegetables. Cut the peppers and the cucumber into thin strips and the avocado into slices. Peel the carrot and cut into thin strips with the peeler.

2.  Heat some sesame oil in a pan. Beat the eggs in a bowl and whisk. Add 3 tablespoons of sake, 1 teaspoon of soy sauce, 2 teaspoons of sugar and a little salt and stir well.

3.  Put 1/3 of the egg mixture into the hot pan. As soon as the egg freezes, roll it up to the middle. Put the egg mass on the vacated area again and make sure that it runs under the rolled egg.

4.  Wait for the egg to freeze and roll in again - this time in the other direction. Place the rest of the egg mass on the vacated area, wait until it stops and roll up completely.

5.  Take the rolled omelet out of the pan and cut into slices. Set everything aside.

6.  Mix 5 tablespoons of rice vinegar, 2 tablespoons of sesame oil and 2 tablespoons of soy sauce and season with the ginger powder. Toast the sesame seeds in a pan without oil.

7.  Spread the rice on bowls (e.g. cereal bowls) and garnish with the vegetables and omelet. Spread the vinegar-oil-sauce mixture over it. Finally sprinkle the roasted sesame over it and serve.

# BEEF WITH ONIONS AND SUGAR SNAP PEAS FROM THE WOK

## INGREDIENTS FOR 6 PORTIONS

- 1.4 kg of beef fillet
- 3 tbsp of vinegar (japanese sushi vinegar)
- 4 tsp of heaped food starch
- 8 tsp of soy sauce
- 2 tbsp of honey
- 1 bottle peanut oil
- 6 large carrots
- 4 large vegetable onions
- 6 fret spring onions
- 200 g of sugar snap
- 1 large chinese bulb of garlic
- 1 glass of bamboo shoot
- 2 pinches of chili flakes
- 2 teaspoons of pepper, freshly ground black
- 1 bunch leaf parsley, fresh
- ¼ liter of broth
- ¼ liter of cream
- 350 g of basmati rice, approx. 2 large cups

# PREPARATION

Total time approx. 1 hour 20 minutes

1.  Remove tendons and fat from the fillet of beef, cut the meat into thin 3 cm strips and place in a container. Mix the sushi vinegar, 4 tablespoons of peanut oil, the soy sauce and honey, and the cornstarch in a bowl with a hand whisk. Then mix well with the strips of meat in the container and put the meat in the fridge for 1.5 hours to marinate.

2.  Cook the rice as usual.

3.  In the meantime, cut the carrots into 5 cm strips, peel, cut in half and quarter the butcher onions and remove the individual onion skins. Wash the sugar snap peas, cut off the ends of the stems and cut the pods in half. Peel and chop the bulb of garlic. Wash the parsley and chop it with a sharp knife. Cut the spring onions into 0.5 cm rings.

4.  Heat a shot of peanut oil in the wok (the oil is hot enough if bubbles form on a wooden spoon). Sear the meat in several stages for two minutes, remove from the wok and let it rest.

5.  Fry the carrots in a wok with a little peanut oil and remove them, then add the sugar pods, onion skin and spring onions and fry. Add half of the garlic and fry. Add the chili flakes and the bamboo shoots.

6.  Now the meat can be mixed with the resulting juice and all ingredients in the wok, only add the black ground pepper with the remaining garlic at the end. Simmer briefly on a low heat, pour in the broth, a little soy sauce and a little dash of cream, then combine with a little brown cornstarch as you like.

7.  Serve with parsley sprinkled with the rice.

# SASHIMI BOWL

## INGREDIENTS FOR 4 PORTIONS

- 500 g of sushi rice
- 80 ml of rice vinegar
- Avocado
- 4 spring onions
- Cucumber
- 4 tbsp of sesame seeds, toasted
- 250 g of salmon, raw, in sushi quality
- 250 g of tuna, raw, in sushi quality
- 100 ml of soy sauce, mild
- 4 tsp of wasabi paste

# PREPARATION

Total time approx. 1 hour 35 minutes

1. Cook the sushi rice according to the package instructions. Then pour the rice vinegar over it. Refrigerate.

2. Cut all other ingredients into small pieces and prepare them.

3. Fill four bowls with the rice to serve. Spread the remaining ingredients on the rice and sprinkle with toasted sesame.

4. Serve with soy sauce and wasabi paste.

5. Pickled ginger and freshly chopped coriander go well with it. If you like, you can also add fresh cubed mango to the bowl and add a dash of lime to the avocado.

# POKÉ BOWL

## INGREDIENTS FOR 3 PORTIONS

- 2 discs of tuna
- 1 cup of sushi rice (approx. 200 - 250 ml)
- 1 cup of soybeans, fresh (approx. 200 - 250 ml), frozen
- 1 tbsp of sesame, black, toasted
- 150 g of wakame (algae salad goma wakame), frozen, seasoned
- ½ chili pepper, fresh, red, medium hot
- Ginger, not too fresh
- 15 tbsp of teriyaki sauce
- Spring onions

# PREPARATION

Total time approx. 2 hours 50 minutes

1.  Cook the sushi rice according to the package instructions, then let it cool in a flat bowl.

2.  Thaw and fry the tuna, then salt and pepper and let cool. Then tear into bite-size pieces. Drizzle with half of the teriyaki sauce, place in a Tupper jar and chill for at least 2 hours.

3.  Cook frozen soybeans until they are bite-proof in salted water for about 5 - 10 minutes, then drain and let cool.

4.  Cut the chili and spring onion into the finest rings and the ginger into fine cubes. Simply thaw the seaweed salad.

5.  Then e.g. Use mason jars for portioning. First pour rice into a glass, then pour in the seaweed salad and the other ingredients, the tuna last. Sprinkle with the sesame seeds and drizzle with 2 - 3 tablespoons of teriyaki sauce.

# JAPANESE STYLE BOWL

## INGREDIENTS FOR 2 PORTIONS

- Cod fillet with skin
- 300 g of sushi rice
- 2 small spring onions
- Onion, red
- ½ tsp of sesame oil
- ½ tsp of yuzu juice or lime juice
- 1 teaspoon of mirin
- 1 teaspoon of soy sauce
- ½ avocado, ripe
- Nori blatt (green mat - crispy seaweed)
- 1 pinch of smoked salt, danish
- Chili

# PREPARATION

Total time approx. 20 minutes

1.  Clean the fish and fry briefly on the skin side.

2.  Prepare the vegetables: Cut the red onion into thin slices. The spring onion in fine strips. Cut the avocado into 1 cm cubes. Mix the sesame oil, yuzu juice, soy sauce and mirin for the marinade.

3.  Cut the fried fish into bite-sized pieces and marinate briefly with the avocado and marinade.

4.  Fill two bowls with 150 g of sushi rice each, put the finely chopped red onions on top and spread the marinated fish and the avocados on top. Decorate with a little spring onion and thin strips of crispy seaweed ("green mat"). If you want, you can add some chili for the hotness.

# BBQ ROLLS

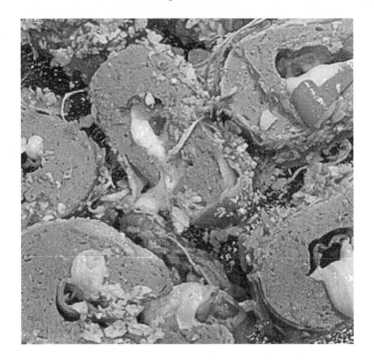

## INGREDIENTS FOR 4 PORTIONS

- 12 discs of bacon
- 500 g of ground beef
- 2 teaspoons of salt
- 2 teaspoons of pepper
- 1 teaspoon of paprika powder, sweet
- 1 teaspoon of paprika powder, spicy
- 1 tbsp of barbecue sauce for ground beef
- 4 chili pepper (jalapenos)
- 1 piece of cheese
- 1 bottle of barbecue sauce to spread on
- ½ bag of nacho

# PREPARATION

Total time approx. 1 hour 30 minutes

1. Season the ground beef according to taste with salt, pepper, paprika powder and barbecue sauce. Place twelve slices of baron overlapping on the sushi mat and spread the ground beef evenly over the bacon. Halve, core and place the jalapenos in the middle of the minced meat. Place the strips of cheese on the jalapenos. Roll everything up with the help of the sushi mat.

2. Briefly fry the roll in oil and then put it in the oven at 200 degrees. Brush the roll from time to time with the barbecue sauce and turn it over so that it turns brown on all sides.

3. Crumble the nachos and roll the fried roll in the nacho crumbs, cut open and serve.

# ASIAN FISH BALLS

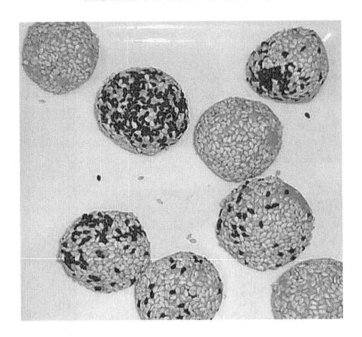

## INGREDIENTS FOR 1 PORTIONS

- 1 can of tuna in its own juice
- 2 teaspoons of wasabi paste
- 3 tsp of mayonnaise
- 1 teaspoon of pickled ginger (sushi ginger)
- 1 teaspoon of soy sauce
- 2 tbsp of sesame

## PREPARATION

Total time approx. 10 minutes

1. Process all ingredients except for the sesame in a food processor to a homogeneous mass. Form 12 small balls out of the mass and roll them in sesame. Place on a plate and serve with ginger and wasabi.

# DESSERT

# SUSHI WITH A DIFFERENCE - SWEET AS A DESSERT

## INGREDIENTS FOR 6 PORTIONS

- 200 g of rice pudding
- 1 liter of milk
- 1 pinch of salt
- 5 tbsp of sugar
- Vanilla bean
- 100 g of grated coconut
- Mango, ripe
- 200 g of strawberries
- 8 kiwi
- Fruit for decoration

# PREPARATION

Total time approx. 1 hour

1. First prepare the rice pudding according to the package instructions with sugar, salt, milk and scraped-out vanilla pulp, it should be sticky and not too firm. While the rice pudding is cooking, grate the grated coconut in a pan over medium heat without fat until it is fragrant and golden brown.

2. Then you wash and cut the fruit. The strawberries are cut into thin slices. 6 kiwi fruit and three quarters of the mango are also cut into thin slices. The milk rice cams are later topped with this fruit.

3. The rest of the mango and the remaining kiwis are cut lengthways so that thicker stripes are created that are as long as possible. These will later be used to fill the sushi rolls.

4. The best way to shape the rice pudding when it is still warm is to let it cool down briefly until it is easy to touch. First you cover a sushi mat (works without it, but it is a little trickier) with transparent film and sprinkle it thickly in the form of a rectangle with the toasted coconut flakes. Width about 10 cm, length as desired and length of the sushi mat. Then spread the rice pudding carefully with the help of a knife. Now place the kiwi and mango strips in the middle of the rice pudding, then roll up the roll carefully using the mat and the transparent film. Everything should be firmly pressed on. Make 2 rolls in this way. Now rest the rolls in the fridge and let them harden.

5. Form the remaining rice pudding into cams with the help of two tablespoons and arrange them on a plate. Cover the cams with the strawberry, kiwi and mango slices.

6. Take the sushi rolls out of the refrigerator and carefully cut them into slices with a sharp knife and arrange them on the plates as well.

7. Can now be decorated with more fruit.

# SWEET SUSHI

## INGREDIENTS FOR 2 PORTIONS

- Carrot
- Apples
- 250 g of strawberries
- 100 g of pistachios, finely ground
- Mango
- 1 bar of leek
- 250 g of rice for sushi
- 1 liter of milk
- 100 g of sugar
- Vanilla bean
- Orange, the grated peel of it
- Lemon, the grated peel of it
- 4 nori sheets
- 250 ml of maple syrup
- 20 g of crème fraiche cheese
- 40 g of sugar
- Ginger, candied, for garnish

# PREPARATION

Total time approx. 45 minutes

1. First boil the rice with the milk, the vanilla pod, the sugar, the orange peel and the lemon peel. Cover and let swell at the edge of the hearth for approx. To cool, spread flat on a large baking sheet and chill.

2. Now prepare various rolls as follows:

3. Maki with carrot and apple (2 rolls)

4. Peel the carrot, grate finely, add a little sugar and drizzle with a little lemon juice. Peel the apples, cut them into rectangular pens of the same size and acidify them slightly with lemon juice. Place the rice on a bamboo mat, place a nori sheet on top and press down a little.

5. Spread rice on the algae leaf and line up the apple sticks 2 cm from the lower edge parallel to the edge. Roll up the sushi roll firmly, loosening the rice from the mat. Then roll in the carrot grated.

6. Maki with strawberries and pistachio (2 rolls)

7. As described above, only use strawberries instead of apples and 100 g pistachios instead of carrots.

8. Nigiri with mango and sweet leek (8 pieces)

9. Cut 8 rice nocks and shape them by hand. Peel the mango and cut the largest possible pieces. Cut 8 slices of the size of the rice noodles into a rectangle and place them on the rice nocks. Wash 2 large leek leaves, briefly brew in very sweet boiling water and quench in ice water. Cut fine green strips from it and wrap the sushi with them.

Pistachio cream:

1. Puree the pistachios, crème fraiche and sugar in the blender.

2. Arrange the sushi rolls on plates and garnish with the candied ginger. Maple syrup and pistachio cream are enough.

# SWEET SUSHI WITH FRUITS

## INGREDIENTS FOR 4 PORTIONS

- 150 g of rice (sushi or risotto rice)
- 100 ml of water
- 150 ml of milk
- 4 tbsp of sugar
- Vanilla bean
- Kiwi
- 100 g of mango
- Strawberries
- 3 tbsp of apricot jam
- 3 tbsp of cocoa powder, unsweetened

# PREPARATION

Total time approx. 30 minutes

1. Place the rice in a sieve and wash until the water becomes clear. Put rice in a saucepan with 100 ml of water, milk and sugar. Halve the vanilla pod, scrape out the pulp, add to the rice and bring to the boil. Reduce the heat and simmer the rice for about 20 minutes, stirring often. Only when the liquid is completely absorbed, put the rice in a bowl and let it cool.

2. Peel the kiwi and mango and cut into strips. Clean and quarter the strawberries. Cut two strips of cling film into rectangles measuring approx. 20 cm x 15 cm and lay them flat on the work surface.

3. Spread the rice over the two pieces of transparent film and spread out into two rectangles. Press the rice down a bit and spread the apricot jam on the rice surface. Distribute the fruit as strips in the lower third of the rice. Using the foil, beat the rice over the fruits and form a roll. Remove the sushi rolls from the foil and roll them carefully into cocoa powder. Then cut into slices and serve.

# RICE PUDDING

## INGREDIENTS FOR 1 PORTIONS

- 250 g of rice (sushi rice)
- 100 ml of milk
- 250 ml of water
- 4 tbsp of honey
- 100 g of peanuts, unsalted, finely chopped
- 100 g of raspberries
- Powdered sugar for sprinkling
- Compote of your choice

# PREPARATION

Total time approx. 30 minutes

1.  Wash rice with cold water. Then put in a saucepan with the milk and water for about 20 minutes and bring to the boil. Then cover and let swell for about 15 minutes.

2.  Sweet rice with honey and divide into 2 portions. Cover a sushi mat with cling film. Approx. Sprinkle half of the area with half of the chopped peanuts. Spread a portion of rice finger-thick on top, press firmly and press in a hollow in the middle of the length. Add half of the raspberries. Roll the rice into a firm roll using the mat.

3.  Prepare a second roll from the remaining rice, peanuts and raspberries. Cool the rolls wrapped in cling film for about 2 hours.

4.  Cut each roll into 6 pieces (the best way to do this is to leave the rice in the cling film, otherwise it will crumble easily - only remove the cling film afterwards).

5.  Sprinkle with powdered sugar and arrange with compote.

# BANANA MAKI SUSHI

## INGREDIENTS FOR 1 PORTIONS

- Banana
- Tortilla, Mexican
- Nutella

## PREPARATION

Total time approx. 5 minutes

1. Brush a tortilla with Nutella, roll the peeled banana into it. Cut the roll into maki pieces about 3 cm wide.

2. Arrange on a plate and garnish with strawberries.

# SUMMER SUSHI

## INGREDIENTS FOR 10 PORTIONS

- 100 g of Sushi rice or milk rice
- 200 ml of Coconut milk
- 2 tbsp of Sweetener of choice, e.g. Rice syrup, cane sugar, xylitol...
- Fruits of your choice, e.g. Banana, melon...

## PREPARATION

Total time approx. 2 hours 5 minutes

1. Wash the sushi rice. Then put in a saucepan with 150 ml coconut milk and simmer with the lid on over medium heat. It took me about 15-20 minutes.

2. Remove from the stove and let it steep for another 5 minutes. Then let the rice cool completely. Then stir in the remaining coconut milk.

3. Take some rice in your hand, form small sausages or balls and place on a plate. Cut the fruit elongated, lay it on top and press it down.

# SUSHI CAKE

## INGREDIENTS FOR 1 PORTIONS

- 300 g of sushi rice
- 5 nori sheets
- 200 g of cream cheese
- Cucumber
- 400 g of salmon fillet (2 pieces of 200 g each)
- Avocado
- Sesame
- Pickled ginger
- Wasabi
- Soy sauce

# PREPARATION

Total time approx. 2 hours 30 minutes

1. Cook the sushi rice according to the package and then process it with rice vinegar, salt and sugar to create the typical sushi rice. Then let the rice cool down a bit.

2. Peel the cucumber. Peel and stone avocados. Cut the cucumber, avocados and salmon fillets into slices.

3. Line the bottom of a 26-inch spring form tin with cling film and then clamp the edge back on.

4. Add an approx. Thumb-thick or, depending on your taste, thick / thin layer of sushi rice and press flat. Tilt this bottom onto a round cake plate. Now spread a thick layer of cream cheese on the rice soil, then put the nori sheets on top. Just cut it so that everything is covered. Spread salmon, avocado and cucumber on top. If the cake has to stand a little, simply drizzle lemon on the avocado, otherwise it will turn brown. Immediately put the bottom in the fridge because of the fish.

5. Create a second base with the remaining sushi rice using a new layer of cling film in the spring form pan. Spread this in the spring form pan with a thick layer of cream cheese and then put the nori sheets on top. Now carefully tip the second floor onto the first floor.

6. Now you can decorate: sesame, the remaining nori leaves, wasabi, ginger and leftover ingredients. The imagination knows no limits.

7. Use a very sharp or serrated knife to cut and slowly cut carefully. Makes 12 pieces.

8. Serve with the pickled ginger, wasabi and soy sauce. Best to eat with a knife and fork.

# CUCUMBER SUSHI

## INGREDIENTS FOR 25 PORTIONS

- 75 g of sushi rice
- 1½ tbsp of rice vinegar
- ¼ tsp of salt
- ¾ tsp of sugar
- 1 large cucumber
- 2 teaspoons of wasabi paste
- 150 g of smoked salmon (slices)
- 20 g of caviar
- 1 bed of cress

# PREPARATION

Total time approx. 30 minutes

1. Wash the rice in standing cold water, drain on a sieve. Repeat the process until the water remains clear. Put the rice with 100 ml of cold water in a saucepan and let it rest for about 20 minutes. Close the pan tightly, bring the contents to a boil over high heat, let swell for approx. 10 minutes on very mild heat. Take the pan off the stove, put a folded tea towel between the pan and the lid, let it swell for about 10 minutes.

2. Lightly heat rice vinegar, salt and sugar in a small saucepan until the sugar has dissolved. Put the rice in a large bowl and mix in the vinegar thoroughly. Let the rice cool down.

3. Peel the cucumber (leave a few peel strips at will), halve lengthways and core. Spread wasabi paste on the inside of the cucumber halves. Pour rice into the cucumber halves. Cut the salmon into short strips.

4. Cut the filled cucumber halves diagonally into 2–3 cm wide pieces. Put some smoked salmon and caviar on each. Garnish with cress as you like.

# Ramen Cookbook

Quick and Easy Japanese Noodle Recipes
for Everyday to Make with Local
Ingredients

MAGGIE BARTON

# EASY – 15/30 MINUTES

# MISO RAMEN SOUP

## INGREDIENTS FOR 2 PORTIONS

- 4 mushrooms (fresh or dried shiitake mushrooms)
- 2 spring onions
- ¼ sheet of nori sheets
- 100g of tofu for soups
- 50g of bean sprouts
- 100g of noodles (ramen or other egg-free asian noodles for noodle soup)
- 2 cloves of garlic
- 1 tbsp. Of oil (neutral)
- ¼ tbsp. Of chili flakes
- 600ml of vegetable stock
- 2 tbsp. Of miso

# PREPARATION

Total time: approx. 15 minutes

1.  Soak the dried shiitake mushrooms in a little water for approx. 1/2 hour, and then bring to a boil briefly, let cool and cut into strips. Only cut fresh shiitake into strips. Cut the spring onions into fine rings, the nori into strips, and the tofu into cubes.

2.  Chop the garlic and fry in the vegetable oil. Before it turns brown, add miso and chili flakes and pour in the vegetable stock.

3.  Cook the ramen or other pasta al dente in boiling water according to the package. Then drain well and spread it over two large soup bowls. Fill up with the miso broth and garnish with shiitake mushrooms, spring onions, bean sprouts, tofu and nori strips.

# MISO SOUP

## INGREDIENTS FOR 2 PORTIONS

- 600ml of water
- Dashi (instant, amount according to the package for 2 servings)
- 2 tbsp of spice paste (miso, light)
- 100g of tofu (in small cubes)
- 2 spring onions (cut into rings)
- 10 sheets of wakame (dried)
- 6 mushrooms (shiitake, dried, cut into fine strips)
- 100g of salmon fillet (alternatively beef fillet, in fine strips)
- 100g of noodles [japanese (udon, soba, etc.) Cooked, possibly shredded]
- 1 tbsp of chives
- Fish sauce or soy sauce
- 1 egg (whisked, at will)

# PREPARATION

Total time: approx. 20 minutes

1. Heat the water with dashi in a larger saucepan; add the tofu cubes and shiitake strips (it is best to cut them with scissors). And let them cook for about 10 minutes. Add onion rings and simmer for another 5 minutes. Add salmon fillet or beef fillet strips and the whisked eggs as desired, cook for 2-3 minutes.

2. Stir in miso paste with a little soup and add cooked noodles and Wakame leaves to the soup, then boil it again. Season to taste and serve sprinkled with chives.

3. Fish stock can also be used instead of water and dashi. For taste reasons, I would only use vegetable or meat broth in an emergency - it is a fish-soy-based soup.

4. The individual insoles can be varied or left out. With all the trimmings, you get a stew that goes as the main course; only with tofu, shiitake, spring onions, egg and/or Wakame can the soup be served very well as part of a Japanese meal. As a warm addition to sushi, the 'stripped down' soup also tastes very good.

# TRADITIONAL MISO RAMEN

## INGREDIENTS FOR 1 PORTION

- 100g of ramen noodles or chinese noodles without eggs
- Oil
- 1 glove of garlic
- Sambal oelek or chili
- 200ml of broth
- 2 tbsp. Of miso paste
- ½ glass of mung bean sprouts
- 2 small disc of roast pork (cooked)
- 3 surimi-stäbchen
- ½ small dose of corn
- Spinach leaves, thawed (portioned) or 2 seaweed leaves
- 1 spring onion

# PREPARATION

Total time: approx. 15 minutes

1. Cook ramen noodles according to the package instructions.

2. Heat the oil in the saucepan. Add garlic and sambal oelek. Before it turns brown, add the broth and stir in the miso paste.

3. Rinse the mung bean seedlings with water and put them briefly in the broth, as well as the roast pork and the Surimi sticks, so that they become warm.

4. Cut the spring onions into small pieces.

5. Place the noodles in a large bowl; arrange everything in a circle except the spring onions. Pour in the broth from the center (let it get really hot again beforehand). Finally, put the spring onions in the middle.

Note:

- This soup can also be modified and, for example, topped with half an egg, broccoli, mushrooms or the likes can be used.

# FAST MISO RAMEN

## INGREDIENTS FOR 4 PORTIONS

- 1 onion
- 2 cloves of garlic
- 1 piece of ginger
- Soy sauce
- Rice wine (optional)
- 2 liters of vegetable broth or chicken broth
- Miso paste (approx. 1 - 2 tbsp.)
- 300g of ramen noodles without egg
- Oil for frying
- For the topping:
- 1 spring onions
- Some mushrooms
- 250g of chicken breast
- Sesame oil
- Chili flakes
- 4 eggs

# PREPARATION

Total time: approx. 30 minutes

1. Cut the onion, ginger, and garlic very finely and fry in a saucepan with a little oil. Deglaze with soy sauce and broth and bring to a simmer. Add the miso paste - preferably through a small sieve, as it will not dissolve easily. Season with a little rice wine and soy sauce. The broth can be used directly or continue to simmer for 10 to 20 minutes.

2. Cook the pasta separately according to the package instructions. Do not add to the broth.

3. Now prepare the toppings. Cut the spring onion. Clean and fry the mushrooms. Marinate the chicken breast with soy sauce and oil, then fry. Boil the eggs for 7 minutes and then put them in ice water so that they are still soft when served.

4. Place the pasta in the serving bowls. Then pour in the broth and spread the toppings on it. The toppings can be varied at will, depending on what you have at home.

# MISO UDON SOUP WITH SILK TOFU

## INGREDIENTS FOR 4 PORTIONS

For the soup:

- 1½ liters of vegetable stock
- 6 tbsp of miso paste
- 3 tbsp of soy sauce
- 3 tbsp of agave nectar
- 2 tbsp of ginger
- 1 tbsp of algae (dried)
- 1 tbsp of garlic powder

Also: (for the insert)

- 400g udon noodles (thick)
- 300g of silken tofu
- 200g of broccoli florets
- 200g of spinach
- 2 spring onions
- 2 carrots

# PREPARATION

Total time: approx. 20 minutes

1.  Bring the soup ingredients to a boil in a saucepan except for the miso paste. Turn the stove down to medium temperature and stir in the miso paste.

2.  Slice the carrots and add to the soup with the broccoli florets and cook for 5 minutes. Cut the silk tofu into pieces, add to the soup, and cook everything together for another 5 minutes.

3.  In the last minute, stir in the spinach and spring onions, and spread everything on bowls.

# FAST RAMEN NOODLES

## INGREDIENTS FOR 2 PORTIONS

- 2 packs of ramen noodles, instant
- 2 spring onions

For the dressing:

- 2 tbsp of soy sauce
- 2 tbsp of chili flakes
- 1 tbsp of rice wine vinegar
- 1 tbsp of agave nectar

## PREPARATION

Total time approx. 15 minutes

1. Cut the spring onions into slices and set the green part aside. Pour boiling water over the white portion and pasta and let it steep for 5 minutes. Then pour off.
2. Mix the ingredients for the dressing and stir it into the pasta. Divide it into 2 bowls and mix with the green part of the spring onions.

# RAMEN NOODLES SOUP

## INGREDIENTS FOR 4 PORTIONS

- 1 tbsp of sesame oil
- 1 shallot (in fine rings)
- 1 clove of garlic, finely chopped
- 100g of shiitake mushroom (in strips)
- 1 chili pepper (green, seeded, finely chopped)
- 1 stem of lemongrass (the inside, finely chopped)
- 1 liter of vegetable stock
- 3 tbsp of soy sauce (light)
- 150g of pasta (ramen)
- 100g of chinese cabbage (in fine strips)
- Coriander

## PREPARATION

Total time: approx. 30 minutes

1. Let the oil warm up in a pan. Add the shallot and all ingredients up, including lemongrass and steam for about 3 minutes. Pour in the broth and soy sauce and bring to a boil. Add the Chinese cabbage and the noodles, cook for about 3 minutes until they are al dente.
2. Spread in soup bowls, garnish with a little coriander.

# RAMEN NOODLES WITH CHICKEN

## INGREDIENTS FOR 1 PORTION

- 1 handful of noodles (ramen noodles) or glass noodles
- 2 spring onions
- Chili powder
- Chicken breast fillet, or beef, cut into small pieces
- Beef broth, or chicken broth
- Sesame oil
- Soy sauce
- Rice vinegar

# PREPARATION

Total time: approx. 20 minutes

1. Cook the pasta in salted water and drain.

2. Cut the spring onion into small rings and fry until translucent, then add the meat and cook.

3. Heat the broth, season with chili, soy sauce, and rice vinegar. Place the broth in a high bowl and put the noodles in so that they protrude above the broth. Carefully place the mixture from the pan over it and cut another spring onion into rings, put them on top. Pour sesame oil over it and serve.

# FAST WANNABE RAMEN

## INGREDIENTS FOR 1 PORTION

- 1 pack of noodles
- 1½ kg cop of plum wine, peach wine, or mirin (shot glass or egg cup full)
- 1 tbsp of miso paste, light
- 1½ tbsp of cane sugar
- 1 egg (cooked)
- 2 small sliced cucumber (snack cucumbers)
- 1 pinch of parsley (frozen, or fresh. If available, you can use chives or spring onions)
- Soy sauce
- Pepper
- Oil

# PREPARATION

Total time: approx. 17 minutes

1. Put some amount of water in a saucepan according to the package, together with the miso paste, cane sugar (or normal sugar), plum wine, seasoning mix of the pasta (if included) and the cucumber. When the water starts to a boil, add the pasta and cook according to the length of the pack.

2. Prepare an appropriate bowl by adding a few dashes of soy sauce, a little pepper, and oil to the bottom of the bowl. Peel, halve and set the egg aside.

3. Put the finished pasta with the broth in the bowl, drape the egg on it and mix with a little parsley, chives or similar. Decorate (spring onions).

Note:

- The ingredients such as egg and the vegetables can be varied with z. B. strips of chicken, carrots, peas, scrambled eggs, or other.

# SIMPLE RAMEN WITH PAK CHOI

## INGREDIENTS FOR 1 PORTION

- 2 tbsp of chicken broth (instant)
- ½ liter of water (hot)
- Ginger
- 1 cloves of garlic
- 1½ tbsp of soy sauce
- 2 tbsp of mirin
- 100g mie noodles (instant)
- 1 pak of choi
- 5 mushrooms or other mushrooms
- 1 chicken breast fillet
- 1 egg

# PREPARATION

Total time: approx. 30 minutes

1.  Mix the chicken broth with the hot water. Cut the ginger and clove of garlic into small pieces and heat them in soy sauce and mirin. Boil the egg and cook the noodles in the chicken broth according to the package instructions.

2.  Then pour the chicken broth with noodles through a sieve over soy sauce, mirin, ginger, and add a clove of garlic so that the two mixes together.

3.  Cut the chicken breast fillet into approx. 1cm thick slices and fry in a little fat, soy sauce, and mirin. Chop the pak choi and mushrooms, and sweat them.

4.  Place the noodles in a bowl, arrange the pak choi, mushrooms, the boiled halved egg, and chicken breast fillet on top, and pour the broth over it.

# SPICY TANTANMEN RAMEN

## INGREDIENTS FOR 2 PORTIONS

- 1 tbsp of olive oil or other oil
- 1 onion
- 1 carrot
- 2 cloves of garlic
- 4 shiitake mushrooms, dried
- 1 liter of water
- 1 tbsp of vegetable broth (instant)
- 1 tbsp of miso paste
- 1 pack of dashi powder
- 1 shot of almond milk (almond drink)
- 2 tbsp of tahini
- 2 tbsp of sambal oelek
- 2 tbsp of sesame oil
- 2 tbsp of soy sauce
- 2 pack of ramen noodles
- Sesame for sprinkling

# PREPARATION

Total time: approx. 30 minutes

1.  Soak the shiitake mushrooms in hot water for 5 minutes. In the meantime, cut the onion roughly so that you can still grasp it well with chopsticks (e.g. B. eighth).

2.  Cut the carrots diagonally into long, 2mm thick slices. Peel the garlic and press on with the knife side.

3.  Fry the shiitake mushrooms, onions, garlic, and carrots in a saucepan with oil on medium heat until they are light brown. A light brown layer should form on the bottom of the pot. Warning, don't let it go black!

4.  Add the water and season with instant vegetable broth, miso paste, and dashi powder. If available, and season to taste. Let the soup simmer gently until the carrots are done.

5.  In the meantime, cook and drain the pasta according to the package instructions.

6.  Prepare 2 soup bowls until the noodles are ready. Whisk 1 teaspoon of sesame paste, 1 teaspoon of Sambal Oelek, 1 teaspoon of sesame oil, and 1 teaspoon of soy sauce with a whisk - by the way, this smells incredibly good.

7.  Fish out the carrot slices and mushrooms out of the soup for decoration. Cut the mushrooms into strips.

8.  Stir the dash of milk into the soup. Spread the soup on the 2 bowls and whisk well with the whisk. Add the pasta to the soup, decorate with carrots, mushrooms. and sesame seeds.

# RAMEN NOODLES WITH PORK

## INGREDIENTS FOR 4 PORTIONS

- 200g of pork
- 1 bar of leek
- 100g of mushrooms (shitake mushrooms)
- 50g of bean sprouts
- 1 piece of ginger (walnut-sized)
- 800ml of broth (miso broth, alternatively chicken broth)
- 250g of noodles (udon noodles)
- 1 chili
- Soy sauce
- ½ bundle of coriander

# PREPARATION

Total time: approx. 20 minutes

1. Cut the pork and sear for approx. 5 minutes on both.

2. Cut the leek into rings, quarter the mushrooms, and shower off the sprouts. Finely chop the ginger and chili pepper, and bring to a boil in the broth with about 3 tablespoons of soy sauce. Then add the leek and cook over medium heat for about 10 minutes. Reduce the heat further and let the mushrooms and sprouts steep for another 5 minutes. Season again with soy sauce.

3. Boil the pasta than arrange the pasta and meat on plates or in bowls. Pour the soup over it and decorate with finely chopped coriander.

# SPICY RAMEN SOUP WITH MUSHROOMS

## INGREDIENTS FOR 3 PORTIONS

- 200g of tofu (japanese, fried)
- 2 liters of vegetable stock
- 2 tbsp of soy sauce
- 3 tbsp of sesame oil
- 1 onion
- 1 carrot
- ½ small cabbage
- 50g of peas, frozen
- 50g of shiitake mushroom
- 100g of bean sprouts
- 1 chili pepper (red)
- 4 tbsp of miso paste
- ½ tbsp of kampot pepper (red, freshly ground)
- ½ tbsp of pepper (black, freshly ground)
- 240g of ramen noodles

# PREPARATION

Total time: approx. 35 minutes

1.  Bring the vegetable broth to a boil with soy sauce and sesame oil, and cook the ramen noodles in the broth in 4 minutes. Take out and keep warm.

2.  Peel the carrot, use a spiral cutter to make strips and shorten to 1cm. Cut pointed cabbage into narrow strips and shorten to 2cm. Peel the onion and cut it into cubes. Dice the shiitake mushrooms.

3.  Cut the tofu into strips and fry in a pan without oil, remove and keep warm with the ramen noodles.

4.  Cook the carrots, onions and pointed cabbage in the broth for 15 minutes. Now add the bean sprouts, shiitake mushrooms, and peas, then cook for another 5 minutes. Chop the chili finely and add to the broth with the pepper and bring to a boil.

5.  Take the pot off the stove and stir the miso paste into the soup.

6.  Spread the noodles on bowls, pour the soup over them and garnish with the tofu.

# SPICY RAMEN NOODLES SOUP

## INGREDIENTS FOR 2 PORTIONS

- 1 liter of chicken broth
- 1 stem of lemongrass
- 1 piece of ginger root
- 4 tbsp of soy sauce (approx. Plus something to taste)
- 80g of ramen noodles
- 300g of chinese cabbage
- 75g of sugar snap
- 1 spring onion
- Lemon juice

For the topping:

- Salt
- 1 of chili pepper (fresh, cut into thin rings)
- Some spring onion (cut into thin rings)
- Sesame

# PREPARATION

Total time: approx. 30 minutes

1. Peel the ginger and chop very finely (it should be about 1 heaping tablespoon).

2. Cut the Chinese cabbage into fine strips, cut the pods in half, and cut the spring onions into rings. Halve the lower light part of the lemongrass lengthways.

3. Simmer broth, lemongrass, ginger and soy sauce in a saucepan for about 8-10 minutes. Add the ramen noodles and cook for 2 minutes. Add Chinese cabbage, sugar snap peas and spring onions, mix everything and cook for about 5 minutes.

4. Season with soy sauce, a little lemon juice, and a little salt if necessary and serve hot.

5. If you want, you can spread the soup on plates and sprinkle with fresh spring onion rings, chili rings and sesame seeds roasted dry in the pan.

# JAPANESE RAMEN NOODLES SOUP

## INGREDIENTS FOR 1 PORTION

- 500ml of water
- 2 tbsp of chicken broth powder (to taste)
- Soup noodles
- 2 eggs
- 1 handful of cherry tomatoes
- 1 shot of mirin (alternatively a little pinch of sugar)
- Soy sauce
- Butter or similar for roasting
- 1 nori sheet (crushed)

# PREPARATION

Total time: approx. 15 minutes

1. Bring the water to a boil; add broth, vermicelli, mirin and soy sauce. Cut the nori sheet into small pieces, you can hold it a little over the warm stovetop, then it becomes brittle and you can easily crumble it. Put in the soup.

2. While the pasta is cooking (stir occasionally so that nothing sticks to the bottom of the pot), fry the eggs with a little butter in the pan over low heat as fried eggs. The eggs should be thorough, but ideally, the egg yolk should still be liquid. If you don't like it that way, you can, of course, fry the fried eggs even longer. Halve the tomatoes and briefly fry them in the pan.

3. When the noodles are soft enough, season the soup, and if necessary, season with soy sauce. Then put the soup in a bowl. As soon as the eggs are ready, carefully slide them into the soup with the tomatoes, if possible without damaging the egg yolk.

4. Depending on the dosage, the soy sauce and nori leaves can be quite flavor-intensive, so it is advisable to first take a little less of both and then season them if necessary.

# SOBA NOODLES WITH TOFU

## INGREDIENTS FOR 2 PORTIONS

- 250g of japanese noodles (soba noodles)
- 300g of tofu (sliced)
- 1 lemon, grated zest and 1 tablespoon of juice
- 3cm of ginger root (grated)
- 1 tbsp of syrup (agave syrup)
- 1 tbsp of cayenne pepper
- 1 tbsp of salt
- 1 shot of rice vinegar
- 1 shot of soy sauce
- 2 tbsp of sesame oil
- Coriander green, chopped
- 5 spring onions (cut into thin rings)
- ½ cucumber (seeded and cut into thin slices)
- ½ bell pepper (red, cut into thin slices)
- Sesame seeds, toasted

# PREPARATION

Total time: approx. 20 minutes

1. Mix the lemon zest with the ginger, agave syrup, cayenne pepper and salt for the dressing. Add lemon juice, rice vinegar, and soy sauce and stir well. Add sesame oil and whip up the dressing with a mixing stick.

2. Cook the soba noodles until bite-proof and quench under cold water. Fry the tofu brown on both sides in a cast iron grill pan, and briefly fry the peppers.

3. Mix the soba noodles with coriander, spring onions, bell pepper, cucumber and 2/3 of the dressing. Spread on two plates, place tofu on each, drizzle with the remaining dressing and sprinkle with sesame.

4. All kinds of salad go well with this.

# SOBA WITH VEGETABLES

## INGREDIENTS FOR 2 PORTIONS

- 250g of noodles, soba noodles (japanese buckwheat noodles)
- 500g of mixed vegetables, frozen (e.g. Peas and carrots)
- 200ml of water
- 1 tbsp of ginger powder
- 5 tbsp of soy sauce
- Lemongrass, to taste
- 1 tbsp of cumin
- 2 tbsp of spice mix (chinese 5-spice powder)
- Salt and pepper (to taste)
- 1 tbsp of berries (red pepper berries)

# PREPARATION

Total time: approx. 15 minutes

1. Place the frozen vegetables with the spices and water on the stove and cook.

2. At the same time, cook the pasta in plenty of salted water according to the package instructions.

3. Drain the pasta in a sieve and add to the vegetables. Mix well and serve.

# SOBA NOODLES WITH PAK CHOI AND MUSHROOMS

## INGREDIENTS FOR 3 PORTIONS

- 150g of Soba Noodles (Japanese Buckwheat Noodles)
- 3 cups of water
- 300g of Pak choi
- 5 large Mushrooms (brown)
- 1 large Onion
- 3 tbsp of hoisin sauce
- 1 tbsp of teriyaki sauce
- 1 tbsp of fish sauce
- ½ tbsp of Paprika powder (noble sweet)
- ½ tbsp of Pepper (ground)
- Salt
- Chili powder
- 100ml of water
- 1 tbsp of Sesame oil or other oil

# PREPARATION

Total time: approx. 30 minutes

1. First, bring the 3 cups of water to a boil in a saucepan, reduce the heat and simmer the soba noodles in them according to the package. Pour into a colander and spray cold. Put aside.

2. Peel the onion and cut it into medium-sized cubes. Wash the pak choi and cut it into strips about 1.5cm wide. Set the leaves aside separately from the stems. Clean the mushrooms and cut them into strips about 0.5cm wide.

3. Heat the sesame oil in a wok. Add onions and stir-fry for about 2 minutes. Add the teriyaki and fish sauce and stir well. Then add the cut stalks from the Pak Choi and let it cook for 2 minutes. Then add the mushrooms and stew for another 3 minutes.

4. Then add approx. 100ml of water and stir well with the hoisin sauce. With the paprika powder, pepper and salt, who like to taste hearty chili powder. Add the drained soba noodles and mix everything well. Let it warm up.

5. The dish can be prepared for vegetarian if the fish sauce is omitted.

# SOBA NOODLES WITH LIME AND PEANUT DRESSING

## INGREDIENTS FOR 2 PORTIONS

- 225g of pasta (soba), optionally another type of pasta
- 2 pak choi (or savoy cabbage or swiss chard)
- 1 small cucumber
- 1 lime
- 2 spring onions
- 1 clove of garlic
- 1 bunch mint
- 50g of peanuts
- 6 tbsp of soy sauce
- 30g of peanut butter
- 20g of honey
- 1 chili pepper (dried)
- 1 tbsp of vegetable oil

# PREPARATION

Total time: approx. 20 minutes

1.  Rub the peel of the lime, squeeze out the lime. Finely chop the peanuts. Finely dice the garlic.

2.  Place the soy sauce with peanut butter, add half of the peanuts, the grated lime peel, and the juice of the squeezed lime, honey, garlic, chili and oil in a tall vessel and mash them finely with a mixing stick. Season with salt and pepper to taste.

3.  Wash the pak choi, remove the stalk and cut into bite-size pieces. Cut the spring onions into fine rings. Finely chop the mint leaves. Quarter the cucumber lengthways and cut into 5mm pieces.

4.  Cook the pasta according to the package instructions. Then put the Pak Choi in the pot and let everything soak in the water for a minute. Drain the soba noodles with pak choi and mix with the peanut dressing in the pot used previously. Add the spring onions, cucumber, remaining peanuts, and mint to the saucepan and stir.

# YAKISOBA WITH VEGETABLES

## INGREDIENTS FOR 2 PORTIONS

- 1 pack of noodles, wide (japanese wheat noodles)
- 1 pack of butter vegetables (frozen)
- Soy sauce or mushroom or teriyaki sauce (asia shop)

# PREPARATION

Total time: approx. 15 minutes

1. Cook the pasta according to the package instructions.

2. Put the buttered vegetables in a saucepan and cook.

3. Arrange the pasta on a deep plate, spread the buttered vegetables on top and drizzle with the sauces to taste.

# YAKISOBA WITH SHRIMPS

## INGREDIENTS FOR 4 PORTIONS

- 500g of japanese noodle, yakisoba noodle (wheat noodle, not buckwheat noodle)
- 200g of cut pork or chicken (into 4 cm pieces)
- 150g of shrimp (washed, deveined, peeled)
- 250g of white cabbage (cut in julienne)
- 1 carrot (cut into strips)
- 1 onion (cut into half rings)
- 1 piece of ginger (approx. 2-4 cm, fresh, finely grated)
- 6 tbsp of sauce (sosu, yakisoba sauce)
- 4 tbsp of soy sauce (light japanese)
- 4 tbsp of sake
- 10g of bonito, dried flakes (katsuobushi)
- Algae, dried (aonori)
- 5 tbsp. Of oil (soybean oil or sunflower oil)
- Japanese mayonnaise

# PREPARATION

Total time: approx. 30 minutes

1. Cook the pasta according to the package instructions, rinse thoroughly with ice-cold water and drain well.

2. Now let the oil get hot in a wok, in a pan or on a teppan (use a little oil on a teppan) and fry the meat and the prawns for about 3 minutes. Now fry the onion. As soon as the onion rings are glassy, add the ginger and carrots and fry for about 2 minutes, stirring constantly. Finally, fry the cabbage until it is tender.

3. Now add the drained pasta and fry for another 2 minutes. Be careful not to turn the pasta often, as they must be browned well, but do not let them burn. Now add the soy sauce and sake, and mix well. Finally, add the Sosu and stir together for another 4 minutes.

4. Arrange immediately on a platter, garnish with mayonnaise, sprinkle Aonori and Katsuobushi over it and serve.

# UDON NOODLE SOUP

## INGREDIENTS FOR 2 PORTIONS

- 4 packs of noodles (udon noodles)
- ½ surimi, japanese kamaboko
- 10g of spring onion (thin)
- 1.2 liters of dashi
- 4 tbsp of mirin
- 5 tbsp of soy sauce
- 0.4 tbsp of salt

# PREPARATION

Total time: approx. 30 minutes

1. Cut the Kamaboko into approx. 5mm wide slices. Remove the roots of the spring onions and cut the spring onions diagonally into thin pieces.

2. Put the dashi in a saucepan and bring to a boil over medium heat. Add the mirin and soy sauce. Salt, bring to a boil again and then remove from the heat.

3. Fill a saucepan with water and bring the water to a boil. When the water boils, add the Udon noodles and cook with stirring (e.g. with chopsticks). After boiling the water again, pour the Udon noodles into a colander and let them drain.

4. Place the noodles in small bowls with the Kamaboko and spring onions. Pour over the broth

# UDON NOODLES SOUP WITH CHICKEN

## INGREDIENTS FOR 2 PORTIONS

- 175g of udon noodles, fresh
- 100g of chicken breast fillet without skin
- 2 pak choi (baby pak choi)
- 1 carrot
- 50g shiitake mushroom, fresh
- 1 shallot (peeled, finely diced)
- 1 clove of garlic, peeled, finely diced
- ¼ tbsp of ginger, fresh, peeled, finely diced
- Sesame oil, light
- 500ml of vegetable broth or chicken broth
- 1 tbsp of miso paste, light
- 1 spring onion
- Soy sauce (light)

# PREPARATION

Total time: approx. 30 minutes

1. Cook the Udon noodles according to the package instructions, pour them into a sieve and let them drain. Cut the chicken into strips. Divide the pak choi, apart from the inside, into individual leaves, wash, and separate the green and white, possibly cut a little smaller. Peel the carrot, cut into julienne. Clean the shiitake mushrooms, remove the stems, cut the caps into slices. Clean and wash the spring onions and cut the white and green into rings separately.

2. Heat the oil in a saucepan; braise the shallot, the white Pak Choi and the spring onions and the garlic. Deglaze with the broth, add meat and shiitake, cook on low heat for five minutes. Mix the miso paste with a little hot broth in a small bowl, add to the saucepan, and do not let it boil. Add the Pak Choi greens, the carrot strips and the noodles, let them steep briefly, season with soy sauce and serve sprinkled with spring onion greens.

# UDON NOODLES SOUP WITH SPINACH

## INGREDIENTS FOR 2 PORTIONS

- 600ml of vegetable stock
- 2 shallots
- 2 cloves of garlic
- Ginger (fresh)
- 1½ tbsp of soy sauce
- 1½ tbsp of mirin
- 1 large carrot
- 150g of udon noodles, pre-cooked
- 100g of baby spinach
- 2 spring onions
- 1 shot of white wine vinegar
- 2 eggs (very fresh)

# PREPARATION

Total time: approx. 30 minutes

1. Peel the shallots, ginger, and garlic, and dice finely. Let it soak in the broth with soy sauce and mirin over medium heat for three minutes. Peel the carrot, slice at an angle, add to the broth and cook for another three minutes.

2. Add the Udon noodles and cook according to the package instructions for about two minutes in the soup. Add the washed baby spinach and the cleaned and sliced spring onions shortly before the end of the cooking time. Drop the spinach together and season to taste.

3. At the same time, heat water in a saucepan with a dash of white wine vinegar. Beat the eggs one by one in a cup and carefully pour it into the hot water. Use a spoon to pull the egg whites around the yolk. Approximately poach for 3-4 minutes, lift out of the water and drain briefly. Serve in the soup.

# UDON NOODLES WITH EGG AND SPRING ONIONS

## INGREDIENTS FOR 1 PORTION

- 1 pack of udon noodles
- 1 egg
- 2 stems of spring onions

For the soup:

- 300ml of water
- 1½ tbsp of dashi, instant
- 1½ tbsp of soy sauce
- ½ tbsp of mirin
- 1 tbsp of sake

Extra:

- Pepper (japanese)
- Spice mix (togarashi)

# PREPARATION

Total time: approx. 25 minutes

1. Wash the spring onions, cut them into bite-size pieces (approx. 2-3 cm) and mix with the whisked egg.

2. Put all ingredients for the soup in a saucepan and simmer on medium heat. If necessary, wash the Udon noodles, and add them to the boiling soup until they are ready.

3. Fry the prepared egg mixture in a pan. Serve the noodle soup and the finished egg mixture and sprinkle with pepper (preferably Japanese pepper) or Togarashi spice mixture if necessary.

# UDON NOODLES WITH MUSHROOMS

## INGREDIENTS FOR 4 PORTIONS

- 250g of noodles (udon)
- 2 tbsp of sunflower oil
- 1 onion (red, cut into rings)
- 1 toe of garlic (crushed)
- 450g of mixed mushrooms (e.g. Shiitake, oyster mushrooms, brown mushrooms)
- 350g of chinese cabbage (or pak choi)
- 2 tbsp of sherry (sweeter)
- 6 tbsp of soy sauce
- 4 spring onions (cut into rings)
- 1 tbsp of sesame seeds (toasted)

# PREPARATION

Total time: approx. 30 minutes

1. Place the pasta in a large bowl and pour boiling water over them so that they are covered. Let it soak for 10 minutes or according to the package. Then drain thoroughly.

2. Heat sunflower oil in a large wok. Put the red onions and garlic in the wok and stir pan for 2-3 minutes. Add the mushrooms and continue stirring for about 5 minutes until cooked. Add Chinese cabbage or pak choi, noodles, sherry, and soy sauce to the wok. Mix all ingredients and stir pan for 2-3 minutes until the liquid boils.

3. Place pasta with mushrooms in preheated bowls and sprinkle with spring onions and toasted sesame.

# UDON NOODLES PAN WITH TERIYAKI BUTTER

## INGREDIENTS FOR 2 PORTIONS

- 200g of udon noodles
- For the sauce: "teriyaki butter sauce"
- 1 clove of garlic
- 1 pinch of thyme
- 75ml of teriyaki sauce
- 1 shot of soy sauce
- 1 teaspoon of honey
- 3 small pieces of butter (cold)
- For the vegetables:
- 1 pak choi
- 2 carrots
- 1 small  zucchini
- 1 handful of sugar snaps
- 1 paprika
- 1 onion
- Oil for frying
- If possible; cashews
- Salt and pepper
- Sugar

# PREPARATION

Total time: approx. 30 minutes

1. In the beginning, the teriyaki butter sauce can be prepared. To do this, put a little oil (I use coconut or peanut oil) in a small saucepan and press the garlic clove with a garlic press or cut it into small pieces and add it to the saucepan. Then sprinkle in the thyme and let it sauté briefly. Now pour everything with the teriyaki sauce and soy sauce and let it simmer.

2. The Udon noodles can be cooked at the same time.

3. Quarter the pak choi, peel the carrots and cut them into sticks. Wash the sugar snap peas well. Cut the bell pepper into strips and the zucchini into pencils. Halve the onion and then cut into rings.

4. Put oil in a pan. Briefly fry the pak choi, carrot sticks and sugar snap peas over high heat, season with salt, pepper, and sugar. Drain the Udon noodles and also briefly fry them. Reduce the heat and put the onions in the pan. Cover the pan with a lid and steam cook the contents of the pan for about 10 minutes. After 5 minutes add the peppers and zucchini.

5. In the meantime, turn off the hotplate of the saucepan and let the sauce cool down briefly. Then add 1 teaspoon honey and 3 small pieces of cold butter and stir. Let the sauce thicken for 2 minutes.

6. Now remove the lid from the pan and stir in the teriyaki butter sauce. Allow to pull through for 5 minutes over low heat.

7. Serve the dish with crushed cashew nuts

8. If you like meat in your meal, you can simply fry it in the pan at the beginning and leave it until the end.

# UDON NOODLES WITH ASPARAGUS AND MUSHROOMS

## INGREDIENTS FOR 2 PORTIONS

- 300g of udon noodles, pre-cooked
- 300g of asparagus, greener
- 150g of shiitake mushroom (fresh, alternatively mushrooms)
- 2 cloves of garlic
- Ginger
- 2 spring onions (lean)
- 2 tbsp of soy sauce
- 2 tbsp of rice vinegar
- Sugar, brown
- 1 tbsp of food starch
- Japanese spice mix (shichimi togarashi)
- Salt and pepper
- Oil

# PREPARATION

Total time: approx. 30 minutes

1.  Cook the Udon noodles in slightly boiling salted water for about
    two minutes, and drain it very well.

2.  Wash asparagus, peel in the lower third, and cut into pieces. Clean
    the shiitake and cut into slices. Peel the cloves of garlic and ginger,
    dice very finely. Clean and wash the spring onions, cut the white
    and green into rings separately.

3.  Mix the soy sauce, rice vinegar, sugar and cornstarch with 5
    tablespoons of cold water.

4.  Heat a little oil in a pan, fry the noodles briefly, then remove and
    set aside. Fry the shiitake; add the asparagus after about 3 minutes,
    then add garlic, ginger and the white of the spring onions and
    steam briefly. Add the pasta and the cornstarch mixture, bring to a
    boil once. Season with soy sauce, pepper, and Shichimi Togarashi
    and serve garnished with the spring onion green.

# UDON NOODLES WITH MISO SAUCE

## INGREDIENTS FOR 4 PORTIONS

- 600g of udon noodles (fresh or pre-cooked, alternatively spaghetti)
- 500g of ground beef
- 1 leek
- 3 spring onions
- 2 cloves of garlic
- ¼ cucumbers
- 250g of miso paste (50:50 light and dark, otherwise only dark)
- 80g of ginger
- 8 tbsp of soy sauce
- 200ml of sake
- 50 ml of mirin (alternatively sake or water)
- 3 tbsp of sugar
- Salt and pepper
- Oil for frying

# PREPARATION

Total time: approx. 30 minutes

1. Wash the leek, shake well and dry, cut in half lengthways and cut into fine strips. You can also cut it first and then wash it in a colander under running water, this is easier. Then peel the ginger and cut as finely as possible. I usually make fine strips, but you can also grate it. Peel and finely chop the garlic. Combine these three ingredients.

2. Wash the spring onions too. Cut off the upper green part, and if desired, cut into rings. Cut the rest of the onions into thin strips. Wash the cucumber, cut in half and then cut into thin pieces, strips or quarters.

3. Put some oil in a pan or ideally a wok and heat briefly. As soon as the oil is warm, add the leek, garlic, and ginger, and then fry briefly until it starts to smell. Then add the minced meat and fry until crumbly. Season with a little pepper.

4. Mix the sake, mirin, miso paste, soy sauce, and sugar, and then pour over the chop and let it boil down until it thickens - this takes about 8-10 minutes.

5. Add the pasta and stir briefly again in the sauce. If you take packaged Udon noodles, simmer for about 2 minutes. If the pasta is already pre-cooked, heat it up briefly in the sauce.

6. Either sprinkle the cucumbers and spring onions on the plate or fold in just before you take it off the stove, then leave on the stove for a maximum of 1 minute so that the cucumber remains crisp.

# UDON NOODLES WITH LEEKS AND SHRIMPS

## INGREDIENTS FOR 4 PORTIONS

- 400g of noodles (udon), japanese
- Salt
- 4 liters of water
- 3 onions (diced)
- 250g of leek (cut into rings)
- 200g of carrot (grated)
- 50g of ginger root (grated)
- 100g of radish (grated)
- 4 tbsp of oil
- 250g of shrimp (uncooked, released)
- 4 tbsp of soy sauce
- 4 tbsp of sauce (sweet-sour), finished product
- 2 tbsp of sesame

# PREPARATION

Total time: approx. 30 minutes

1.  Cook the Udon noodles in 4 litre of salted water in about 8 minutes.

2.  Heat the oil in a large pan; fry the onions, leek, carrots, and ginger in it for about 3 minutes. Drain the pasta. Mix with the prawns and the two sauces under the vegetables and cover. Let it simmer over low heat.

3.  Roast the sesame seeds without fat in a pan and sprinkle them with the radish rasps over the pasta.

# COLD UDON NOODLES WITH SOY SAUCE DIP

## INGREDIENTS FOR 1 PORTION

- 1 pack of udon noodles, approx. 200 g
- 1 tbsp of soup spice (maggi)
- 1 tbsp of soy sauce
- 1 tbsp of dashi or vegetable broth
- 1 tbsp of mirin
- 1 piece of cucumber
- Lovage
- Tarragon
- Chili powder

# PREPARATION

Total time: approx. 20 minutes

1. Place the Udon noodles in a microwave oven, pour a little water over them and let them cook for 3 minutes at 700 watts.

2. Stir in a cup of water, Maggi, soy sauce, dashi, and mirin - and add an ice cube if necessary to cool it.

3. Stir the Udon noodles until they are loose. Drain and quench with cold water until cool, then pour into cold or ice water.

4. Slice the cucumber. Place the Udon noodles on a plate and sprinkle with chili. Serve decorated with cucumber slices, tarragon, and lovage.

5. The dip can either be poured over the pasta or the pasta can be dipped.Add carrot, bamboo shoots, spring onions and everything your heart desires – as they will all go well with this.

# FRIED UDON NOODLES WITH BEEF

## INGREDIENTS FOR 1 PORTION

- 200g of udon noodles
- 130g of beef (cut into thin slices)
- 1 handful of bean sprouts
- 1 handful of chinese cabbage, cut into strips
- 5g of mu'er mushrooms (dried)
- 1 clove of garlic (chopped)
- 2 discs of ginger root (chopped)
- 1 shallot (finely chopped)
- 1 tbsp of oyster sauce
- Salt and pepper

# PREPARATION

Total time: approx. 30 minutes

1.  Pour boiling water over the Mu'er mushrooms, let them soak and cut into strips.

2.  Pour boiling water over the Udon noodles and leave for 2-3 minutes. Let it brew until it's soft and you can get it apart.

3.  In a little oil, briefly fry the chopped garlic and ginger together with the shallot and then add the thin strips of beef, fry very briefly, add the Mu'er mushrooms and season with a little salt. Afterwards, briefly fry the noodles and then add the Chinese cabbage, the soy sprouts, the soy sauce, the oyster sauce and 2-3 tablespoons of water, season to taste with salt and pepper and only continue to fry for a very short time.

# NOODLES SOUP WITH CHICKEN

## INGREDIENTS FOR 3 PORTIONS

- 1 liter of water (1 to 1 1/4 liter)
- 2 dice of broth
- 3 spring onions
- 2 large carrots
- 300g of chicken meat
- 3 pack of noodles (japanese instant noodles)
- Salt and pepper
- Curry
- Soy sauce
- 1 egg (boiled)

# PREPARATION

Total time: approx. 25 minutes

1.  Wash the spring onions, cut into thin slices. Peel the carrots, cut twice lengthways, then cut into thin (minimum approx. 5mm) triangles. Free the chicken from tendons and then cut into bite-size pieces.

2.  Bring the water to a boil in a saucepan and dissolve the stock cubes in the water. Some stock cubes are more intense than others, so add as much to the water as it says on the package and then season. Cook the carrot corners until they're almost done.

3.  Add the spring onions and the chicken, salt, pepper and add some curry. Taste again and again. You can season a little more because afterward the noodles are added, which take away some of the taste (or salt).

4.  After the meat is cooked, add the pasta and cook. Then season again with soy sauce (I take about 4 sprinkles). When the pasta is done, season again and serve. If you like, you can also cut a boiled egg.

# BAMI GORENG INDONESIAN NOODLES

## INGREDIENTS FOR 3 PORTIONS

- 250 g of chinese egg noodles
- 1 leek
- 1 glass of bamboo shoot
- 1 large carrot
- 150g of cauliflower
- 1 glass of mushrooms (sliced or fresh)
- 200g of chicken fillet, fried, cut into pieces
- Soy sauce (wok sauce)
- Curry powder
- Soy sauce
- Soy sauce, japanese (teriyaki)
- Spice mix (chinese spice)
- Spice mix (tandoori masala)
- Cumin
- Ginger
- 1 tbsp. Of sauce (sweet-sour sauce)

# PREPARATION

Total time: approx. 30 minutes

1.  Prepare the pasta according to the package instructions.

2.  Cut the leek into thick slices. Heat a dash of wok sauce in a pan and braise the leek in it. Quarter the carrot and cut into slices. Drain the bamboo shoots and add to the leek. Steam briefly, then mix in the carrot pieces, pour some wok sauce over them, season with curry, stir and let simmer for a few minutes. Cut the cauliflower into small florets, mix in and let everything simmer gently. Then drain the mushrooms, add them and let them heat up.

3.  Drain the finished pasta, add immediately and chop a little. Next, mix in the pieces of meat and mix everything vigorously. Season with soy sauce, teriyaki sauce, sweet-sour sauce, and the spices, and stir again.

# CHINA NOODLES

## INGREDIENTS FOR 2 PORTIONS

- 250g of chinese egg noodles
- 1 bar of leek
- 1 bell pepper (red)
- 1 handful of bean sprouts, fresh
- 200g of chicken breast
- Soy sauce (dark, japanese)
- 200ml of chicken broth
- Pepper
- Spice mix (chinese spice)
- Oil

# PREPARATION

Total time: approx. 25 minutes

1. Cook, pour and set aside the pasta according to the package instructions. Cut the leeks and peppers into pieces that are not too large. Do not dice the chicken breasts too large either. Approximately prepare 200ml of chicken broth.

2. Heat a wok or large pan. Add neutral oil. Now sear the meat vigorously in portions, season properly with salt and pepper, remove from the pan and keep warm. Then put the vegetables in the pan and fry with some color. Then add the meat again, as well as the drained, not too soft-cooked pasta. Add a lot of soy sauce (you should try your taste).

3. To keep the Asia pan nice and moist, deglaze with chicken broth so that the soy sauce can nestle nicely around the pasta. Season with a little Chinese spice and pepper. If the whole thing is too neutral, add more soy sauce. Do not worry; it will not be too salty since salt has been omitted overall.

# NOODLES WITH EGG

## INGREDIENTS FOR 1 PORTION

- 1 pack of pasta (noodles, of your choice)
- 1 egg
- 1 spring onion
- ½ carrot
- 1 shot of soy sauce
- 1 tbsp of sesame oil
- 1 tbsp of chili sauce (sweet, at will)
- ½ clove of garlic (at will)
- 1 tbsp of fried onions (alternatively peanuts or roasted sesame)
- Sambal oelek (at will)

# PREPARATION

Total time: approx. 20 minutes

1. Cook the pasta in a small saucepan as shown on the package instructions. Keep about 1 or 2 tablespoons of the ramen broth, drain the pasta and pour the remaining broth away.

2. Wash the carrots and spring onions, cut the carrots into the finest possible sticks (e.g. you can peel them into thin slices with a vegetable peeler, then cut them into small strips), cut the spring onions into small slices. If you like, you can chop the garlic finely. Put the drained pasta back in a saucepan, add the onion, carrot and possibly garlic, and then mix well.

3. In a small bowl, whisk together the egg with the soy sauce, the cooled broth, (and if you like) sweet chili sauce and Sambal Oelek, and mix the egg mixture thoroughly with the pasta so that all the pasta are covered with egg. If the egg stops a bit, it is not a problem.

4. Add soybean oil in a pan and sauté the egg and noodle mixture in it until the egg is stocked everywhere, but not too dry. Sprinkle with the roasted onions, peanuts or sesame seeds and serve.

# NOODLES SOUP WITH SAUERKRAUT

## INGREDIENTS FOR 6 PORTIONS

- 450g of noodles
- 500g of sauerkraut
- 400g of pork neck (cut into short thin strips)
- 3 large ones of tomatoes
- 3 liters of vegetable stock
- 1 toe of garlic
- 1 tbsp of heaped sugar
- 3 tbsp of soy sauce
- 1 tbsp of sesame oil
- 2 tbsp of fish sauce
- 3 tbsp of tomato paste
- 1 tbsp of paprika
- 2 tbsp of heaped flour
- 1 tbsp of heaped five-spice powder
- 1 tbsp of heaped ginger
- 1 pinch of chili flakes
- Salt
- Oil (neutral)

# PREPARATION

Total time: approx. 30 minutes

1. Peel the onion and cut it into large pieces, chop or press the garlic. Mix the finely chopped meat with flour, and dice the tomatoes.

2. Cook the pasta with one minute less cooking time.

3. Fry the meat in a high pan with neutral-tasting vegetable oil for about 3 minutes and then remove from the pan. Sauté onions with garlic until lightly browned. Add the sauerkraut and fry for 5 minutes.

4. Add all the spices. Put the pasta and broth in the pan (if you take instant broth, you can take the pasta water). Add the tomatoes and the meat and let everything simmer for 2 to 3 minutes, season to taste, then serve immediately.

# JAPANESE FRIED NOODLE WITH MINCED MEAT

## INGREDIENTS FOR 4 PORTIONS

- 500g of minced meat (mixed or beef)
- 300g of noodles (soba or mie noodles or spaghetti)
- Saltwater
- 1 piece of ginger (fresher)
- 2 cloves of garlic (fresh)
- 1 chili pepper, fresh
- 2 spring onions
- 50ml of soy sauce (japanese)
- 50ml of sake
- 1 tbsp of sesame oil
- Salt and pepper
- 2 tbsp of rapeseed oil

# PREPARATION

Total time: approx. 30 minutes

1. Peel and grate the ginger (so you have no tough fibers). Chop the garlic finely (fresher does not leave such a strong stench, but a lot of aromas) and the chili (this is important to me), and then put aside. Wash, clean and cut the spring onions into fine rings and also set them aside.

2. Loosen the minced meat in a bowl and spread 3 tablespoons of soy sauce, 3 tablespoons of sake and 1 tablespoon sesame oil over the meat. Season with pepper, mix thoroughly and leave for 15 min. to let go.

3. During this time, let some noodles soak in salted water, pour off shortly before the end of the specified cooking time (collect 3 - 4 tbsp. of pasta water). Quench with cold water to complete the cooking process.

4. Let the rapeseed oil (or another neutral oil) heat up in a wok or high pan. Briefly fry the ginger, chili, and garlic so that the flavors get through, then reduce the heat a bit and fry the minced meat. Spread the meat finely and crumbly. Try some minced meat, add soy sauce if necessary.

5. When the meat is crispy, add the remaining sake and let the alcohol evaporate. Then add the pasta with the pasta water, swirl everything (or mix with tongs). Fry for 3-4 minutes. Season to taste with salt. Arrange in a pretty bowl and sprinkle the spring onions over it.

# SPICY NOODLES WITH CHICKEN

## INGREDIENTS FOR 4 PORTIONS

- 300g noodles
- 1 leek
- 1 eggplant
- 6 mushrooms
- 1 small dose of corn
- 500ml of tomato happened
- 4 chicken breast fillet
- 2 tbsp of sauce (wok sauce)
- 50 ml of vegetable stock
- 1 tbsp of heaped sambal oelek
- 1 tbsp of curry powder
- 1 tbsp of rosemary
- 1 tbsp of spice mix (chinese spice)
- 2 tbsp of soy sauce (japanese teriyaki sauce)
- Oil

# PREPARATION

Total time: approx. 25 minutes

1. Cook the pasta. Cut the meat into pieces, fry in a little oil and set aside.

2. Cut the leek into thick rings, quarter the eggplant, cut into coarse slices and halve them again if necessary. Drain the corn and cut the mushrooms into slices.

3. Heat the vegetables in the wok sauce and stir until they are brown. Deglaze with the vegetable broth and mix in the Sambal Oelek. Drain the pasta and mix in with the meat and the tomatoes. Heat, season with the spices and mix vigorously.

4. Finally, season with the teriyaki sauce, stir again and serve.

# BUCKWHEAT NOODLES WITH VEGETABLES

## INGREDIENTS FOR 4 PORTIONS

- 250g of noodles (soba noodles - japanese buckwheat noodles)
- 250g of potato, firm cooking
- ½ head savoy cabbage, small (approx. 300 g)
- 3 liters of vegetable stock
- 1 teaspoon of salt
- 12 sheets of sage
- 1 large onion
- 5 toes of garlic
- 60g of butter
- 4 tbsp of rapeseed oil
- 50g of parmesan cheese (grated)
- Salt and pepper

# PREPARATION

Total time: approx. 30 minutes

1.  Peel the potatoes and cut them into small cubes. Clean the savoy cabbage and cut it into fine strips. Heat the vegetable broth, cook potatoes and savoy cabbage on low temperature for 15-20 minutes.

2.  In the meantime, chop the sage, cut the cloves of garlic into thin slices and finely dice the onion. Heat the butter and oil together and fry the onion, garlic, and sage in the mixture until golden.

3.  Now add the pasta to the vegetables in the broth and let them cook at a high temperature until they are al dente as instructed. Then pour on a sieve.

4.  To serve, alternately place the pasta and cheese on the plates and pour the sage butter over them. Finally, sprinkle with pepper.

# SOBA ROLLS

## INGREDIENTS FOR 1 PORTION

- 1 tbsp of oil
- 125g of tuna (sushi quality or tuna fillet)
- 100g of noodles (soba noodles) broken into pieces
- Water
- 1 spring onion (the green), cut into thin rings
- 1 tbsp of soy sauce (light)
- ½ tbsp of rice vinegar
- Wasabi powder
- 1 tbsp of ginger (pickled, finely chopped)
- 6 nori leaves (toasted)
- ½ cucumber (peeled, cut into fine strips)

# PREPARATION

Total time: approx. 20 minutes

1. Heat the oil in a pan and fry the tuna fillet on all sides for 6 minutes until it is almost done. Cut into stripes.

2. Cook the soba in a saucepan with boiling water until bite-proof, drain and rinse under running cold water. Drain thoroughly. Mix the soba carefully with spring onion, soy sauce, rice vinegar, a little wasabi, and pickled ginger.

3. Divide the pasta into 6 equal portions. Place a nori sheet with the glossy side down on a sushi mat and spread 1 portion of the pasta mixture on the lower third. Put a sixth of the cucumber on top, put a layer of tuna on top.

4. To roll up, fold the mat upwards, starting with the ingredients at the end and turning in the nori edge while rolling. Pull the mat up and continue rolling with even, light pressure. Moisten the top edge of the sushi roll with water to seal it. Push back the ingredients sticking out on the sides. The edges may look unfinished.

5. Remove the roll from the mat and cut it into 4 equal pieces. Arrange the sushi on a plate with the cutouts facing down. Do the same with the remaining ingredients.

# PASTA WITH SLICED PORK AND PEAS

## INGREDIENTS FOR 2 PORTIONS

- 500g of pork
- 1 tbsp of soy sauce
- 1 tbsp of mirin (japanese rice wine)
- 1 handful of peas (frozen)
- 1 tbsp of rapeseed oil or sunflower oil
- Salt and pepper
- Garlic
- 200g of noodles

# PREPARATION

Total time: approx. 25 minutes

1. First stir a soy sauce and mirin into a teriyaki sauce (ready-made one is also available) and cook the noodles.

2. Fry the sliced pork in the oil. When the meat is almost cooked, deglaze with the previously mixed sauce. You can also add a little salt, pepper, and garlic to taste.

3. Finally, add a handful of frozen peas and the poured pasta, and swirl everything in the pan again properly. When the peas and the noodles are hot, the pork chop is done.

# JAPANESE LEEK PASTA

## INGREDIENTS FOR 4 PORTIONS

- 500g of penne
- 2 leeks
- 500g of ground beef or mixed minced meat
- 6g of dashi
- 100ml of soy sauce
- 2 cloves of garlic
- 2 tbsp of sugar
- 2 tbsp of sake
- 3 tbsp of sesame

# PREPARATION

Total time: approx. 30 minutes

1.  For the noodles, heat a saucepan with water and add dashi, soy sauce, and sake (about half of the stated amount).

2.  Now fry the minced meat in a second saucepan and add the leek, cut into rings about 1cm wide, and fry. After about 5 minutes, when the meat is cooked, press in the cloves of garlic, add soy sauce, sake, and sugar and let it simmer a little. Before adding the pasta to the seasoned water, add about three ladles from the brew to the meat. The sauce can be thickened with cornstarch.

3.  When the pasta is al dente, drain the water and mix the pasta with the minced meat and leek mixture.

4.  The sesame can either be added in this way or briefly browned in a pan and then mixed in. It is also good for decorating the meal.

# JAPANESE BOLOGNESE

## INGREDIENTS FOR 2 PORTIONS

- 400g of ground beef (alternatively soy mince)
- 2 cm of ginger root (fresh)
- 1 bunch of spring onions
- 1 toe of garlic
- 4 tbsp of miso
- 3 tbsp of soy sauce
- 100ml of mirin (alternatively sherry)
- 2 tbsp of dashi (powder)
- 1 tbsp of sugar
- 400g of pasta, (udon, fresh)
- ¼ cucumbers
- 2 tbsp of sesame (white and black)

# PREPARATION

Total time: approx. 30 minutes

1.  Peel and finely chop the ginger and clove of garlic. Cut the spring onions into fine rings and set aside a small portion for the garnish. Wash and core the cucumber and cut into very fine strips about 6 cm long.

2.  Fry the spring onions, the ginger and the garlic in neutral oil in a wok until glassy, then add the ground beef. Continue frying until the meat is cooked. Now stir in the miso paste, the soy sauce, the mirin, the dashi powder, and the sugar and let everything simmer for about 5 minutes at low temperature.

3.  In the meantime, cook Udon noodles according to the package instructions. Spread the cooked pasta in small bowls, put the minced meat sauce on top and garnish with cucumber strips, spring onion rings, and sesame.

# JAPANESE SESAME CHICKEN

## INGREDIENTS FOR 4 PORTIONS

- 500g of chicken breast fillet, in pieces
- 1 pepper (in narrow strips)
- 1 chili pepper (finely chopped)
- 2m. In size carrot (in narrow strips)
- 2 tbsp of pepper (szechuan pepper)
- 10 tbsp of sesame
- 2 cloves of garlic (finely chopped)
- 5 tbsp of soy sauce (sweet, ketjap manis, substitute normal soy sauce)
- 6 tbsp of sesame oil, toasted
- 400g of noodles
- Oil (peanut oil)

# PREPARATION

Total time: approx. 20 minutes

1.  Cook the pasta in a little salted water for 3-5 minutes, drain and set aside. Toast the sesame in a pan without oil, and then set aside.

2.  Let the pieces of meat soak in a saucepan with plenty of lightly boiling saltwater.

3.  Heat the peanut oil in a pan, add the peppers, carrots, garlic, and chili, and fry for 5 minutes, then add the sesame, Szechuan pepper, ketjap manis, the chicken and the sesame oil and stir for another 3 minutes. Possibly add a dash of water.

4.  Arrange with the pasta.

# FRIED JAPANESE EGGPLANT

## INGREDIENTS FOR 2 PORTIONS

- 1 eggplant (japanese)
- 1 clove of garlic
- 2 tbsp of olive oil
- 1 handful of cocktail tomatoes (halved or quartered)
- 2 tbsp of ajvar
- ½ tbsp of thyme
- Salt and pepper from the mill
- 2 packs of pasta such as spaghetti, linguine, or rice
- Mushrooms (or zucchini or onion)

# PREPARATION

Total time: approx. 25 minutes

1. Cut the eggplant into small slices, cut the large slices in half again. You can also use normal eggplant, but the Japanese eggplant is less tart than normal and takes a little less rest.

2. Place the eggplant pieces on a board, sprinkle with salt and let the liquid soak for 5 minutes. In the meantime, prepare a bowl of oil, halve the cloves of garlic and press into the oil with a fork. Now season with a little salt, ground pepper, and add thyme and mix.

3. As soon as the eggplants have formed liquid on the surface, dab with a kitchen towel, then pour into the flavored oil. Mix well, then put on the pasta or rice as usual and cut the cocktail tomatoes.

4. Then heat a coated pan over medium heat. No additional oil is needed since the eggplant is already in place. Fry the eggplant, if you don't like it, take out the garlic. Then add the cocktail tomatoes and mix in the Ajvar. If necessary, add a small dash of water if it should be more liquid.

5. Drain the pasta or rice and serve everything together.

6. The recipe can be easily expanded with other ingredients that are still in the house. Mushrooms and zucchini, for example, also taste great in the spicy oil. A little parmesan goes well with this meal.

# CHINESE CABBAGE SALAD

## INGREDIENTS FOR 6 PORTIONS

- 1 chinese cabbage
- 1 bunch of spring onions
- 3 packs of ramen noodles
- 100g of almond, planed
- 50g butter
- 1 cup of sugar
- ¾ cup of oil
- ½ cup of soy sauce
- ½ cup of vinegar (5-herb vinegar)
- 1 bell pepper (red, as desired)

# PREPARATION

Total time: approx. 30 minutes

1. Cut the Chinese cabbage into fine strips, cut the onions with green into slices.

2. Chop the ramen noodles with a hammer. Sauté together with the almonds in the hot butter until everything is golden brown. Let it cool down.

3. Make a dressing from sugar, oil, soy sauce, and vinegar. Shake well. Now mix all the ingredients well and let it steep for another 15 minutes.

4. If you still need some color for this salad, you can add a finely chopped red pepper.

# CARBONARA

## INGREDIENTS FOR 1 PORTION

- 1 egg
- 1 egg yolk
- 30g parmesan
- 2 discs of bacon
- 200 g of pasta (spaghetti)
- 2 tbsp of olive oil
- Salt and pepper

# PREPARATION

Total time: approx. 30 minutes

1.  Put egg, egg yolk, parmesan and pepper in a small bowl to taste. Whisk well with a fork.

2.  Cut the bacon slices crosswise into strips about 1.5 cm wide. Fry in a pan, but it shouldn't be made crispy yet.

3.  Cook the pasta according to the package instructions in boiling salted water.

4.  Put the olive oil in the pan with the bacon, heat, and stir. As soon as the oil is hot, remove the pan from the heat. Pour some pasta water into the bacon and stir. Add the ramen noodles and mix. Add the egg mixture. Make sure that you put them on the pasta and not directly on the pan. Stir vigorously.

5.  The heat from the pan turns the egg mixture into a creamy sauce. But if the eggs get too hot, it becomes a kind of scrambled eggs. If necessary, additional pasta water can be added to obtain a smooth but creamy sauce.

6.  Serve sprinkled with parmesan and pepper.

# JAPANESE STEW

## INGREDIENTS FOR 4 PORTIONS

- 500g of minced
- 500g of pasta
- 500g of leek
- 750ml of broth

## PREPARATION

Total time: approx. 15 minutes

1. Fry the chopped tomato paste and bring to a boil with the broth. Then add the spaghetti and leek and simmer for half an hour.

# SPAGHETTI NAPOLI IN JAPANESE

## INGREDIENTS FOR 2 PORTIONS

- 200g of spaghetti
- 3 small sausages (smoked)
- ½ onions
- ¼ bell pepper (green)
- 1 tbsp of oil
- 4 tbsp of ketchup
- Salt and pepper
- 50g of parmesan cheese (greaves)
- Parsley

## PREPARATION

Total time: approx. 20 minutes

1. Cook the spaghetti with a little salt in a saucepan according to the package.
2. Cut the sausages into bite-size pieces. Cut the peppers and onions into thin strips.
3. Heat a large pan with the oil and fry the sausages, peppers, and onions in it for 1-2 minutes. Now add the cooked spaghetti and fry briefly, and then add the ketchup and season with salt and pepper.
4. Arrange the pasta with parmesan and parsley.

# RAMEN BURGER

## INGREDIENTS FOR 2 PORTIONS

- 400g of ramen noodles, alternatively mie noodles
- 2 beef burger patties
- 1 egg
- 1 shot of teriyaki sauce
- Arugula
- Spring onions
- Oil

## PREPARATION

Total time: approx. 30 minutes

1. Prepare the pasta according to the package and let it cool.
2. Then mix with the egg. Heat the oil in the pan, add four palm-sized noodles to the pan and twist. Fry on both sides until golden brown. Then drain on kitchen paper.
3. Now you can prove it: First place the rocket and meat patty on one half of the pasta burger. Then drizzle with teriyaki sauce and top with spring onions cut into rings. Finish with the second half of pasta.

# MEDIUM – 30/90 MINUTES

# TRADITIONAL NOODLES SOUP

## INGREDIENTS FOR 4 PORTIONS

- 600g of chinese egg noodles, thin
- 500g of pork loin
- 4 eggs (boiled, peeled)
- Bamboo shoot
- Sunflower oil or other vegetable oil
- Water
- 1 spring onion (cut into rings)
- 3cm of ginger, freshly peeled and grated
- 100ml of soy sauce
- 50ml of sake
- 1 tbsp of sugar
- 2 liters of water
- 4 tbsp of chicken broth (instant)
- 4 tbsp of soy sauce

# PREPARATION

Total time: approx. 1 hour 30 minutes

1. The meat broth is prepared first. It is best to make them yourself.

2. Heat the sunflower oil in a saucepan and fry the loin (or alternatively lean pork) in it. Add the spring onions, ginger, soy sauce, sake, and sugar and fill with water so that the meat is covered. Now bring everything to a boil, switch it down and let it simmer for about 40 minutes. When the broth is half cooked, add the eggs. So they can take on the color with the meat. After cooking, the meat is cut into small pieces and the eggs cut in half.

Now for the main course:

1. Bring the 2 liters of water to a boil; add the instant chicken broth, the previously prepared meat broth (approx. 100ml) and the soy sauce. Let it simmer on a low flame.

2. Prepare the pasta separately and put them in the serving bowls or plates. Put the soup and eggs on top. Season with salt and pepper, garnish with fresh spring onions and enjoy.

3. The deposits can also vary depending on the season. For example, people like to add bamboo shoots in spring and mushrooms in autumn.

# SOBA WITH MISO SOUP, MUSHROOMS AND BROCCOLI

## INGREDIENTS FOR 2 PORTIONS

- 150g of soba noodles
- 1 liter of water (warm)
- 4 tbsp of miso paste (dark)
- 4 tbsp of soy sauce
- 2 tbsp of rice wine vinegar
- 1 tbsp of sesame oil
- 250g of mushrooms (brown)
- 5 spring onions
- 2 cloves of garlic
- 1 broccoli
- 2 tbsp of ginger
- 1 tbsp of chili flakes

# PREPARATION

Total time: approx. 40 minutes

1. Slice the mushrooms. Cut the broccoli into florets. Slice the spring onions and set the green part aside. Chop the garlic finely.

2. First, cook the soba noodles in a large saucepan for 3 minutes and then pour into a colander and rinse cold.

3. Dry the pot and put it on the stove again. Put some oil in the saucepan and heat. Fry the mushrooms for about 5 minutes and lightly salt them. After 5 minutes, stir in the white part of the spring onions, garlic, and the ginger, then briefly sauté. Dissolve the miso paste in warm water and add the mixture together with the broccoli to the saucepan. Simmer the soup for 10-15 minutes until the broccoli is cooked. Finally, stir in soy sauce, rice wine vinegar, and sesame oil.

4. Spread the pasta on 2 bowls and spread the soup on top. Garnish the soup with the green part of the spring onions and the chili flakes.

# NOODLES SOUP WITH PRAWNS

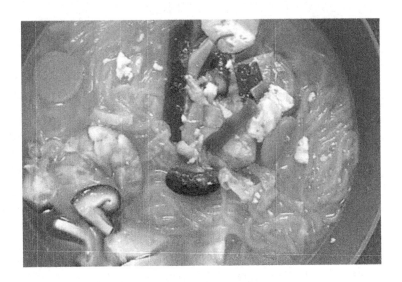

## INGREDIENTS FOR 4 PORTIONS

- 100g of glass noodles
- 8 shiitake mushrooms
- 250g of cod fillet
- 12 king prawns
- 250g of tofu
- 2 carrots (thin)
- ½ head of chinese cabbage (approx. 250 g)
- 2 spring onions
- 1,000 ml of chicken broth (instant)
- 2 tbsp of sherry (dry)
- 3 tbsp of soy sauce
- 1 tbsp of lemon juice
- Cayenne pepper

# PREPARATION

Total time: approx. 40 minutes

1.  Cut the glass noodles into 10cm pieces, scald them with boiling water and let them steep for 2 minutes, then drain.

2.  Clean the mushrooms and cut lengthways into quarters. Rinse fish fillet briefly, pat dry and cut into bite-size pieces. Remove the shell from the shrimp, leave the tailpieces on and gut them.

3.  Cut the drained tofu into 8 cubes. Peel the carrots and slice them into thin slices. Clean, wash, halve and cut Chinese cabbage into strips of about 3cm wide. Clean the spring onions and slice them into thin slices.

4.  Bring the broth to a boil. Add all the ingredients except the onions and let cook for 2 minutes. Finally, season with sherry, soy sauce, lemon juice, and cayenne pepper and sprinkle with the spring onions.

# KIMCHI NOODLES SOUP

## INGREDIENTS FOR 3 PORTIONS

- 350g of white cabbage
- 350g of red cabbage
- 1 leek
- 2 carrots
- 1 zucchini
- 2 cloves of garlic
- 1 piece of ginger root (approx. 3 cm)
- 1 large onion
- 1 glass of kimchi (approx. 400 g)
- 200g of tofu (japanese, fried)
- 2 tbsp of coconut oil
- 2 tbsp of palm oil (red)
- 100g of peas, frozen
- 800ml of vegetable stock (asian)
- 4 tbsp of soy sauce
- 2 tbsp of soy paste
- 2 spring onions
- 2 tbsp of chili flakes
- 150g of ramen noodles
- Sea-salt

# PREPARATION

Total time: approx. 1 hour 15 minutes

1. Clean the cabbage and leek, and cut into strips. Clean zucchini and cut into cubes. Peel and slice carrots. Peel and chop the ginger, onion, and garlic.

2. Thaw frozen peas. Dice Japanese tofu. Heat palm and coconut oil in a saucepan. Braise the ginger, garlic, tofu cubes, and onions. Add the remaining vegetables and braise for another 5 minutes. Sprinkle with the sugar and let caramelize for 1 minute while stirring. Deglaze with the stock and add the Kimchi. Stir in soy sauce and soy paste. Season with the chili flakes. Bring everything to a boil and simmer on a low flame for 45 minutes.

3. Cut the spring onions into thin rings. Prepare the ramen noodles according to the package insert.

4. Place a portion of ramen noodles in a bowl and fill with the soup. Sprinkle with spring onions and serve.

# UDON SOUP WITH MINCED MEAT

## INGREDIENTS FOR 4 PORTIONS

- 500g of ground beef
- 4 packs of udon noodles (fresh)
- 1 zucchini
- 1 eggplant
- 1 bag of beans (green)
- 7 sheets of savoy
- 1 piece of pak choi
- 3 tbsp of thai curry paste, green
- 4 tbsp of sesame (white)
- 1 can of coconut milk (400 ml)
- Soy sauce
- Chili oil
- Sesame oil
- Salt and pepper

# PREPARATION

Total time: approx. 1 hour

1.  Slice the eggplant and quarter it. Cut the zucchini and savoy cabbage into strips. Roast the sesame dry in a coated pan, remove and set aside.

2.  Fry the eggplant slices in sesame oil in a deep pan until they become a little soft. Add zucchini, savoy cabbage, and beans and continue to fry for about 5 minutes.

3.  It is best to sear the ground beef in parallel in a second pan. Crush the sesame seeds with 3 teaspoons of curry paste and mix with the ground beef. Add the ground beef to the vegetables in the deep pan and mix well. Add 1 liter of beef broth and let it boil down. Season with salt and pepper. If you like, you can add a hint of soy sauce and chili oil.

4.  Only add the coconut milk at the end. Let it steep briefly on medium heat. Cook the Udon noodles in parallel.

5.  Arrange everything in a deep plate or bowl. Garnish with pak choi.

# UDON SOUP WITH CURRY

## INGREDIENTS FOR 3 PORTIONS

- 1 pack of noodles (udon)
- Oil
- 1 bunch of spring onions
- 1 onion
- 1 carrot
- 400g of chicken breast fillet or turkey breast fillet
- 2 tbsp of soy sauce
- 500ml of water (possibly more)
- Dashi
- Curry paste
- 1 tbsp of food starch

# PREPARATION

Total time: approx. 40 minutes

1. First, cut the meat into bite-size pieces and put it in a little soy sauce. Clean the spring onions and cut them into rings. Peel and dice the onion and cut the carrots into thin slices.

2. Put a little oil in a wok and first sauté the onions, spring onions and carrots. Then add the pickled meat and fry until the meat is cooked. In addition, prepare the pasta according to the package instructions.

3. Deglaze the contents of the wok with the 2 tbsp. of soy sauce. Add water and dashi. The packaging shows how much dashi belongs in which amount of water, this varies from product to product.

4. Add the curry paste when everything is boiling and dissolve. If the soup is too thin despite the curry paste, simply thicken it with cornstarch. Add the pasta to the soup and serve.

5. Tip: Do not take the round moist Udon noodles, but the dried ones.

# UDON NOODLES SOUP WITH PORK FILLET

## INGREDIENTS FOR 2 PORTIONS

- 750ml of chicken broth (homemade, not an instant)
- 10g dashi (dashi powder, from the asian shop corresponds to 1 small bag)
- Pork
- 2 fret of spring onion (less depending on size)
- 2 eggs (hard-boiled)
- 2 pack of udon noodles (200 g each, fresh)
- Salt and pepper
- Soy sauce

# PREPARATION

Total time: approx. 1 hour

1. Parry the pork fillet, if necessary fold in the flat end a little and tie it together using a kitchen thread so that it does not dry out when seared and in the oven. The fillet is only peppered and salted when it comes out of the oven.

2. Put the fillet in a hot pan and sear well for about 8-10 minutes.

3. Meanwhile preheat the oven to 100 degrees top and bottom heat.

4. Remove the pork fillet from the pan, wrap it in a piece of aluminum foil and put it in the oven for 30 minutes.

5. Boil the pasta in a saucepan according to the package instructions. Drain and quench with cold water, and then spread over two large bowls.

6. Put the chicken broth in a saucepan, mix with the dashi powder and heat. Meanwhile, clean the spring onions and cut them into small rings. Peel the eggs and split them in the middle.

7. After 30 minutes, take the pork fillet out of the oven, add pepper and salt, and then cut into slices about 1cm thick. The juice in the aluminum foil can of course also be added to the broth.

8. Add the soup to the noodles in the two bowls. Then drape the slices of pork fillet along the edge, place 2 egg halves in a bowl and divide the spring onions cut into rings between the two bowls.

9. If you want, you can fry the leek with a little chili instead of the spring onions, deglaze with soy sauce and add to the soup.

10. The recipe is very variable; you can let off steam when it comes to the composition of the soup.

11. The portion is really huge and can be adjusted according to hunger. If there are leftovers from the pork fillet, they can be eaten cold the next day.

# UDON SOUP WITH CHICKEN

## INGREDIENTS FOR 4 PORTIONS

- 400g of udon noodles
- 200g of chicken fillet
- Soy sauce
- 1 shot of sake
- 1 carrot
- 6 shiitake mushroom or similar
- 1,150ml of dashi or other broth
- 100g of spinach
- 2 spring onions
- 3 tbsp of mirin
- 4 eggs

# PREPARATION

Total time: approx. 1 hour

1.  The preparation takes a little time – so you have to be fast with it.

2.  Bring 1.5 liters of water to a boil and let the noodles cook for 10 minutes. Take care that it does not foam. Add a little cold water if necessary and stir from time to time so that the pasta does not stick together. Place the pasta in a colander and cold-chill.

3.  Cut the chicken into bite-size pieces and marinate with a good dash of soy sauce and sake for ten minutes.

4.  Peel and slice the carrot. Clean the mushrooms and cut them into slices about 0.5cm thick. Wash and select spinach. Cut the spring onions into pieces approx. 2.5cm long.

5.  Depending on the firmness or cooking time, gradually add the ingredients to the 1,150ml broth with mirin. First, add the carrot slices. After about two minutes, add the chicken, and after another two minutes, add the mushrooms (if you want to add pak choi or something else, add these ingredients accordingly). Then season with mirin, soy sauce, and pepper.

6.  Now the noodles come in portions in four soup bowls. Spread a few leaves of spinach on top and put the soup on top.

7.  Preheat the oven to 200°C top/bottom heat.

8.  Slide one egg each into a soup bowl and place the ready-to-serve dishes in the oven for about ten minutes until the egg is ripe.

9.  Serve the soup bowls from the oven directly with chopsticks. And remember: in Japan, you can sip while eating soup.

10. Tips: You can still vary the ingredients for the stew. If you like, you can also add Japanese eggplant or Pak Choi.

# UDON NOODLES WITH PEANUTS AND VEGETABLES

## INGREDIENTS FOR 4 PORTIONS

- 400g of udon noodles (fresh)
- 400g carrot
- 250g mushrooms
- 2 fret of spring onions
- Chili pepper
- 100g of peanuts (roasted and salted)
- 1 piece of ginger
- 2 toes of garlic
- 75ml of mirin
- 150ml of sake
- 200ml of beef broth or vegetable broth
- 50ml of soy sauce, preferably japanese
- Five-spice powder
- Honey
- Pepper
- Gravy

# PREPARATION

Total time: approx. 50 minutes

1. Peel and finely chop the ginger and garlic. Cut the chili into fine rings. Peel the carrots and cut them into fine strips or rings. Clean the mushrooms, remove the stems and quarter them. Clean the spring onions and cut them into rings.

2. Briefly fry ginger and garlic in a little oil, then deglaze with beef or vegetable stock, sake, soy sauce, and mirin. The quantities given for the liquids are only approximate values. The amount and composition can vary depending on the taste and sauce requirements, so maybe not at the beginning; do not pour the complete amount of liquid into the pot, but gradually do it if necessary.

3. Add carrots and chilies, and simmer for five minutes, then add the mushrooms and spring onions and simmer for another 3-5 minutes. Season with the five-spice powder and possibly honey and pepper, and if necessary, thicken with sauce binders, depending on how much sauce you have made and how thick you want this sauce to be. Finally, stir the Udon noodles and let them steep for approx. 2-5 minutes, so that they get warm and taste.

4. Serve with the roasted peanuts.

# UDON NOODLES WITH TOFU AND SPINACH IN PEPPER SAUCE

## INGREDIENTS FOR 4 PORTIONS

- 2 handfuls of baby spinach
- 270g of udon noodles
- 200g of tofu
- 1 tbsp of sesame oil

For the sauce:

- 50ml of water
- 6 tbsp of soy sauce
- 3 tbsp of rice vinegar
- 2 tbsp of food starch
- 1 tbsp of pepper
- 3 tbsp of garlic
- 2 tbsp of agave nectar
- 1 tbsp of ginger powder

# PREPARATION

Total time: approx. 40 minutes

1.  For the pepper sauce, dissolve the starch in cold water. Add soy sauce, rice wine vinegar, ginger, agave syrup, garlic and pepper, and use in a blender to make a smooth sauce.

2.  Bring the water to a boil and cook the noodles for 4-5 minutes until they are firm to the bite. Drain the pasta and rinse with cold water to prevent them from sticking together.

3.  Cut the tofu into cubes. Heat some sesame oil in a larger pan and fry tofu until the cubes are brown all around. Remove the pan from the hob, deglaze with a dash of water, add a dash of pepper sauce and swirl the pan through once so that the tofu is glazed all around. Set the tofu aside.

4.  Pour some sesame oil into the pan that has already been used. When the oil is hot, add the pasta and pepper sauce. Fry the noodles with constant stirring until they are completely covered with sauce. Remove the pan from the heat and stir in the spinach and tofu cubes.

5.  Divide the pasta into 4 plates and serve garnished with sesame.

6.  Tip: The amount of tofu and spinach can be varied as desired.

# UDON NOODLES WITH PORK AND VEGETABLES

## INGREDIENTS FOR 2 PORTIONS

- 2 pack of japanese noodles (udon, the fat ones)
- 2 small onion or 1 large one
- 1 zucchini
- 2 potatoes
- 2 toes of garlic
- 300g of pork belly or neck
- 2 tbsp. Of spice paste (black bean paste, heaped tablespoons)
- 2 tbsp. Of potato starch
- Mix water
- Vegetable oil
- 1 teaspoon of sesame oil
- 5 small mushrooms
- 200ml of beef broth or pork broth
- 200ml of water
- Extra: cucumber for garnish

# PREPARATION

Total time: approx. 40 minutes

1.  Cut the onion into eighths and separate the pieces. Cut the zucchini and mushrooms into small cubes, then (if you want, peeled) potatoes and the pork belly into 1-2 cm cubes. Cut or press the garlic very finely and mix the potato starch with a little water. Prepare the pasta according to the package instructions.

2.  Fry the pork belly with a little oil in a wok or large pan for 4-5 minutes until crispy brown. If you want, you can soak up the pork fat with a kitchen towel.

3.  Now add the potatoes, zucchini, onion, and the mushrooms and continue to heat for about 2 minutes. Stir well. Now push the meat and vegetables to the edge so that you have a free area in the middle.

4.  Put 1 tablespoon of oil in this area, wait a little while until it is hot and add the black bean paste. Fry while stirring, turn down the heat, then stir in the vegetables and meat with the paste.

5.  Now add the broth and 100-200ml of water and close the wok with a lid and leave it for 10-15 min. Simmer until the potatoes are done. Now carefully stir in the starch water and continue stirring until you have a thick sauce.

6.  Spread the noodles in bowls; pour a lot of sauce over them. If necessary garnish with a little cucumber and enjoy.

# UDON CHICKEN BREAST WITH

## INGREDIENTS FOR 4 PORTIONS

- 600g of chicken breast
- 2 tbsp of sesame oil
- 150ml of sauce (teriyaki – in my recipe)
- 350g of noodles (udon)
- 2 tbsp of oil (peanut)
- 2 carrots
- 250g of beans (green, as narrow as possible - princess beans)
- 1 bunch of spring onion (the white, cut into fine cubes)
- 1 clove of garlic (cut into fine cubes)
- 1 tbsp of ginger root (grated)
- Salt and pepper
- 1 tbsp of cayenne pepper

# PREPARATION

Total time approx. 45 minutes

1. Triple the data in my recipe for the Teriyaki sauce from the database and slowly reduce it to almost a third of the amount simmering to make the sauce very sticky.

2. Cut carrots and peppers into Julienne with a length of 5cm and cook crispy in peanut oil for 5 minutes. Then mix in the onion, a clove of garlic and the ginger, lightly salt it and leave it to stand for 5 minutes.

3. Blanch beans for 4 minutes, then halve in length and add to the vegetables with the cayenne pepper.

4. Now mix the bite-proof pasta with the vegetables and mix in half of the teriyaki reduction. Turn several times.

5. At the same time, platter the chicken breasts on the thicker side and roast to the point so that they are just through. Brush with the rest of the teriyaki sauce. Finally, lightly salt and pepper. Cut the breasts crosswise into slices and arrange the vegetable mix next to or above the noodle.

# JAPANESE COLD BUCKWHEAT NOODLES WITH DIP

## INGREDIENTS FOR 4 PORTIONS

- 600g of noodles (soba, japanese buckwheat noodles)
- 4 spring onions
- 1 nori sheets
- Wasabi paste (japanese, green, from a tube or powder)

For the sauce:

- 1½ cup of water
- 0.33 cup of sake, alternatively white wine or mild sherry
- 1 tbsp of sugar
- 0.33 cup of soy sauce (japanese)
- 0.33 tbsp of dashi (japanese instant fish broth)

# PREPARATION

Total time approx. 50 minutes

1.  Bring all ingredients for the sauce to a boil briefly, and then simmer for 2-3 minutes over low heat. Cool in a water bath and then refrigerate for at least 30 minutes.

2.  Cut the spring onions into fine rings. If available, cut Nori into thin strips with scissors.

3.  Boil soba in plenty of boiling water according to the package instructions, and then put in a colander and quench ice-cold. Rinse well, and then drain.

4.  Place the pasta in 4 plates (sprinkle with Nori strips if necessary), distribute the sauce in 4 dip bowls.

5.  Everyone mixes spring onions and wasabi (be careful, very spicy) in the dip sauce and dips the noodles (chopsticks-for-chopsticks or fork-for-fork) briefly into the sauce. A typical summer meal in Japan.

# NOODLES WITH FRIED TOFU AND BROCCOLI

## INGREDIENTS FOR 4 PORTIONS

- 200g of broccoli
- Sea-salt
- 200g ramen noodles
- 250g of tofu (japanese fried)
- 6 m in size of mushrooms
- 1 onion (red)
- 2 chili pepper (fresh)
- 1½ tbsp of bean paste, black
- ½ tbsp of five-spice powder
- 3 tbsp of soy sauce, dark
- 2 cloves of garlic
- Peanut oil
- Sesame oil
- 5 stems of coriander

# PREPARATION

Total time: approx. 1 hour 15 minutes

1.  Wash the broccoli, separate the florets and cut them into smaller pieces. Cook the broccoli bite-proof in sufficient saltwater over medium heat for 5-7 minutes. Then pour into a sieve, quench cold and let it drain.

2.  Cook the ramen noodles according to the package instructions, pour them into a sieve and let them drain.

3.  Cut the tofu into cubes. Clean the mushrooms and cut them into thick slices. Peel the red onion and cut lengthways into narrow slices. Halve, clean, core and chop the chilies. Mix the bean paste and five-spice powder with chilies, 2 tablespoons of soy sauce, and vegetable broth. Peel and press the garlic.

4.  Heat sufficient peanut and sesame oil in a wok and fry the tofu all around, salt and remove from the wok. Pour in some oil, then briefly fry the mushrooms and onion while stirring. Add broccoli and stir briefly. Pour in the seasoning broth and mix everything. Cook on medium to high heat for 5 minutes, stirring, until the broth is almost completely boiled down.

5.  Finally, add the ramen noodles and tofu and mix in, continue to stir until the sauce is almost completely absorbed by the ramen noodles and everything is well covered with it, season with the remaining soy sauce.

6.  Decorate with coriander and serve.

# YAKISOBA SALMON

## INGREDIENTS FOR 4 PORTIONS

- 300g of noodles (japanese noodles of your choice, e.g. Soba)
- 300g of vegetables of your choice (e.g. B. Broccoli, zucchini, carrots, baby corn, pak choi, spinach)
- 2 spring onions
- 1 cloves of garlic
- Salt and pepper
- For the fish:
- 4 salmon fillets
- 2 tbsp of marinade (homemade of your choice, e.g. B. Based on soy sauce or lemon juice)
- Sesame (optional)

# PREPARATION

Total time: approx. 40 minutes

1.  Wash the salmon and dry it with kitchen paper.

2.  Heat a pan with tasteless oil over medium heat, add the garlic until the garlic has flavored the oil, and then remove. Add the spring onion and the vegetables, and fry.

3.  Cook the noodles in hot water a little shorter than indicated on the package.

4.  The Japanese use soba noodles, but use whatever you want, but never use Italian pasta.

5.  Put 1 1/2 tablespoons of the pasta water in the pan, this prevents the vegetables from burning, for example, and makes it cook a little faster. Then you put the noodles in the pan and the vegetables that don't need cooking, such as pak choi and spinach. Reduce the heat and season with salt and pepper.

6.  Heat some oil in another pan. Fry the salmon on both sides. It should still be slightly glassy in the middle.

7.  Drape the yakisoba on a plate and add the salmon as you like.

8.  Brush the salmon with the marinade and sprinkle sesame seeds on top.

# SALMON FILLET

## INGREDIENTS FOR 2 PORTIONS

- 2 salmon fillets
- For the marinade:
- 1 lemon (the juice of it)
- 1 lime (the juice of it)
- 2 cloves of garlic
- Pepper (szechuan pepper and japanese mountain pepper, both lemon-heavy)
- 1 tbsp of rosemary
- 1 tbsp of thyme
- 5 tbsp of olive oil (preferably from crete)

For the vegetables: (ratatouille)

- 2 onions (finely diced)
- 1 clove of garlic (finely diced)
- 1 zucchini (finely diced)
- 1 pepper (red, finely diced)
- 4 tomatoes (finely diced)
- Salt
- Sugar
- 2 packs of tagliatelle
- Sea salt (maldon sea salt)

# PREPARATION

Total time: approx. 40 minutes

1.  For the marinade, combine the juice of the fruit, the Szechuan pepper and the remaining ingredients for the marinade and mix with the hand blender. Wash the salmon, pat dry and marinate in a freezer bag with the marinade for several hours (even better overnight) in the fridge.

2.  Preheat the oven to 150 ° C.

3.  Put on the water for the pasta. When it boils, give it plenty of salt (approx. 2-3 teaspoons) and cook the pasta 2-3 minutes less than stated on the package. Then don't be put off! Very important!

4.  Now remove the salmon from the freezer bag and save the marinade. Place a piece of fish on the aluminum foil. Season with Japanese mountain pepper and a little salt and pour 2 teaspoons of the marinade on top, then close the foil tightly. Do the same with the second piece.

5.  For the ratatouille, fry the onion and garlic cubes in olive oil in a pan, then remove from the pan. Then add the paprika and zucchini cubes, sweat in it and let it take a little color. Finally, add the tomato cubes and cook everything.

6.  Put the fish in the aluminum foil on a rack for 10 minutes in the hot oven and cook.

7.  Now season the vegetables with salt and sugar. Add the rest of the marinade to the vegetables and bring to a boil. Season everything well.

8.  Drain the pasta and add to the vegetables, bring to a boil once and finish cooking in the vegetables for about 2-3 minutes.

9.  Now serve the ratatouille pasta on a plate. Place the fish in the foil next to it - open the foil on the table a little, so you can smell the aroma vapor. Sprinkle with a little Maldon Sea Salt Flakes as desired. Serve immediately.

# SHIRATAKI NOODLES WITH MINCED MEAT AND GINGER

## INGREDIENTS FOR 1 PORTION

- 100g of ground pork
- 200g of shirataki noodles
- 1 onion
- 1 tbsp of sugar
- 1½ tbsp of soy sauce
- 1 tbsp of sake
- 1 small piece of ginger
- Oil

# PREPARATION

Total time approx. 45 minutes

1. Cut the onion into thin slices.

2. Drain the Shirataki noodles, rinse and boil for about 3 minutes in hot salt water so that the slightly fishy smell disappears. Peel the ginger and cut it into fine cubes.

3. Heat some oil in a saucepan and fry the ginger in it. Then add the minced meat and fry gray. Deglaze with the sake. Add the onion and shirataki noodles. Stir well so that everything is covered with oil. Add the sugar and braise everything until the onions are translucent.

4. Finally, add the soy sauce and continue cooking until the shirataki noodles have accepted the taste well.

# JAPANESE NOODLE SOUP WITH FRIED TOFU

## INGREDIENTS FOR 2 PORTIONS

- 300g of tofu (natural, firm)
- 2 tbsp of soy sauce (japanese)
- 1 tbsp of mirin
- 2 tbsp of sake
- 4 tbsp of broth (e.g. Dashi)
- 100ml of oil (for deep frying)

For the soup:

- 600ml of broth (dashi), also vegetarian
- 250g of noodles (udon), thick wheat noodles
- 2 spring onions (the green parts)
- ½ tbsp of salt (as needed)
- Soy sauce

# PREPARATION

Total time: approx. 1 hour

1. You can either buy the fried tofu ready or make it yourself. To make it yourself, you wrap the cube-shaped solid tofu with kitchen paper, weigh it down for a quarter of an hour with a chopping board or saucepan so that the liquid it contains is squeezed out. Then cut it into 3-4 mm thick square slices. The ingredients for the marinade are heated in a pan, the tofu slices are put in and the mixture is simmered over low heat until the liquid has evaporated. Carefully turn the slices once.

2. Now wipe the pan dry (or take a new one) and heat the oil, which should be about 1cm high. Three or four slices of tofu are always fried at once, turned once. When the slices have become a little brown, put them on kitchen paper to drain them. With another sheet of kitchen paper, which is placed over it, the excess oil is also removed from the top. The squares are cut into triangles (like fox ears).

3. For the soup, boil the noodles in lightly salted water for 2-3 minutes according to the instructions, briefly brew them in a pasta strainer with cold water and distribute them in two bowls. Add the hot dashi, a couple of tofu slices on top and finally, the green parts of the spring onions cut diagonally into fine rings.

# OTSU SALAD

## INGREDIENTS FOR 2 PORTION

- 340g soba noodles
- 340g of tofu (firm)
- 1 lemon (grated zest of it)
- 1 piece of ginger root (thumb-sized, peeled and grated)
- 1 tbsp of honey
- ¾ tbsp of cayenne pepper
- ¾ tbsp of sea salt
- 1 tbsp of lemon juice (fresh)
- 60ml of rice vinegar (unseasoned, brown)
- 80ml of soy sauce
- 2 tbsp of olive oil
- 2 tbsp of sesame oil (dark, from roasted sesame seeds)
- ½ bundle of coriander green (chopped)
- 3 spring onions (thinly sliced)
- ½ large cucumber or 1 small one (peeled, halved lengthways, cored, cut into thin slices)
- 1 handful of coriander green for garnish
- 4 tbsp of sesame seeds (toasted, for garnish)

# PREPARATION

Total time: approx. 40 minutes

1. Cook the soba noodles in package directions. Then drain and rinse under cold water.

2. Heat a coated pan without fat and roast the sesame seeds until they take on color and spread a nutty scent.

3. Drain, dry, and dice the tofu, then fry in a pan with a lot of oil until crispy and golden brown.

4. Mix lemon zest, ginger, honey, cayenne pepper, and salt for the dressing until it has a mushy consistency. Add lemon juice, rice vinegar, and soy sauce. Finally, add the oils and always stir.

5. Mix the soba noodles, coriander, spring onions, cucumber, and a small part of the dressing in a large bowl. Finally, add the tofu and garnish with the remaining dressing, a few coriander leaves, and the toasted sesame seeds.

# SOY STOREY

## INGREDIENTS FOR 3 PORTIONS

- 200g of noodles (ramen, or mien noodles)
- 1 egg yolk (class m)
- 150g of baby spinach
- 1 clove of garlic
- 10g of ginger
- 7 tbsp of sunflower oil
- 1 tbsp of sesame oil
- 1 tbsp of honey
- 2 tbsp of soy sauce
- Salt and pepper
- Sugar
- 300g of ground beef
- 2 discs of cheese
- 6 tbsp of teriyaki sauce
- 3 tbsp of mayonnaise
- 1 tbsp of wasabi paste
- 1 mini-cucumber
- 1 tomato
- 2 spring onions

# PREPARATION

Total time: approx. 1 hour

1. Cook the pasta in plenty of boiling salted water according to the package instructions. Scare the pasta cold, drain in a sieve and pat dry with kitchen paper. Whisk egg yolk and mix with the pasta in a bowl. Divide the pasta into 4 round molds of approx. 3cm high (diameter 8-10 cm). Cover with cling film, press firmly and - for example, weigh down with a can of tomatoes. Place in the fridge for 20-30 minutes.

2. In the meantime, wash spinach and spin dry. Peel and finely dice the ginger. Also dice the garlic finely. Heat 1 tablespoon of oil, sesame oil, and honey in a pan. Fry the garlic and ginger until golden yellow. Add the spinach and let it collapse. Season with soy sauce, pepper, salt, and 1 pinch of sugar and set aside.

3. Knead the meat with 2 tbsp. of teriyaki sauce and season well with pepper. Form 2 patties from the mass. Mix the mayonnaise and wasabi paste. Cut the cucumber into slices. Slice the tomato. Clean, wash and cut the spring onions into thin strips.

4. Remove the pasta from the molds. Heat 4 tablespoons of oil in a coated pan and fry the pressed noodles on each side for 5-6 minutes. Then drain on kitchen paper and keep warm in the oven.

5. Heat the remaining oil in a pan. Season the patties with salt and pepper and fry on each side for 3-4 minutes. After turning, deglaze with the remaining teriyaki sauce and pour the cheese onto the patties.

6. Place 1 packet of pasta with tomato, cucumber, spring onions, drained spinach, and patties. Drizzle with the mayonnaise and finish with the remaining noodle packages

# GRILL OR BAKE RAMEN PIZZA

## INGREDIENTS FOR 2 PORTIONS

- 200g of ramen noodles, dried
- 2 eggs
- 1 tbsp of sunflower oil
- 250ml of tomatoes (happened)
- 2 tbsp of herbs of Provence

For covering:

- Salami, ham, mushrooms, onions, and olives, etc.
- 300g of gouda (grated)

# PREPARATION

Total time: approx. 50 minutes

1. Put ramen in hot water and soak for three minutes. Drain the water and let the ramen cool. Then mix the two whisked eggs into the ramen.

2. Coat the baking sheet with oil. Layout a thin layer of ramen. Sprinkle a fine layer of cheese on top. Sprinkle the sieved tomatoes over it. Sprinkle with herbs from Provence. Now pour a little cheese over it again.

3. Garnish with a topping (your choice).

4. Bake in the grill at around 350°C until the bottom becomes crispy (can take between 8-15 minutes).

Note:

- The recipe is of course also successful in the oven - it takes a little longer (approx. 200 degrees). Some even fry the ramen pizza in the pan.

# MISO RAMEN WITH SMOKED TERIYAKI

## INGREDIENTS FOR 2 PORTIONS

For the broth:

- 500ml of water
- 250ml of meat soup
- 2 large oranges
- 3 tbsp of soy sauce (light)
- 3 tbsp of oyster sauce
- 2 tbsp of honey
- 1 tbsp of ginger (grated)
- 1 thai chili
- 2 discs of smoked bacon (intense, no black forest ham)
- 2 nori sheets
- 3 tbsp of miso paste
- 2 cloves of garlic
- 1 tbsp of apple cider vinegar (or rice vinegar)

For the meat:

- 400g of meat (as you like; chicken, beef, shrimp, etc.)
- 1 clove of garlic
- 3 tbsp of soy sauce
- 1 tbsp of honey
- 1 large orange
- 1 tbsp of ginger (grated)

Moreover:

- 2 pack of ramen noodles
- For the vegetables:
- 1 small federation of spring onion (fresh)
- 1 bag of bean sprouts, fresh
- 1 bowl of mushrooms (fresh, shiitake mushrooms)
- 50g of carrot (grated)
- 50g of celery (grated)

# PREPARATION

Total time: approx. 1 hour 25 minutes

For the broth:

1.  Bring the water and broth to a simmer. Strip the orange peel away from the oranges. Squeeze the oranges and pour the juice into the boiling broth. Add the soy sauce, oyster sauce, honey, ginger, chili pepper, smoked bacon, nori leaves, miso paste, and 2 pressed cloves of garlic and simmer gently for 45 minutes. Season the broth to taste.

2.  Parry the meat.

3.  Let the broth simmer for another 10 minutes. The broth should taste very strongly sweet-salty-smoky towards the end and almost 1/3 of the actual liquid should have evaporated. Add the vinegar. Then briefly boil the broth and set aside. Season the broth again as it is important that it is very intense. You can continue to taste and add soy sauce, miso paste, and honey. If too much liquid has escaped, add water.

For the meat:

1. Cut the meat into bite-size pieces and cook in the soup for 5 minutes as soon as the soup has boiled down for at least 30 minutes. Then remove the meat again.

2. In a pan, for a marinade; add honey, soy sauce, grated ginger, pressed cloves of garlic, and boil the orange strips of the orange and its juice until a very flavorful syrup is obtained. Briefly turn the cooked meat in it and set aside for marinating.

3. According to the instructions, cook the ramen noodles. It is important not to add salt.

For the vegetables:

1. Wash everything and cut into pieces or strips as desired. Wash and set the bean sprouts aside. The spring onions, mushrooms, carrots, and celery are just suggestions. You can also add other vegetables here. Pak choi or sugar snap peas and other crunchy vegetables are particularly suitable. Please make sure that you can eat the corresponding vegetables raw, otherwise, prepare them beforehand.

2. Warm-up two deep bowls. Add the pasta evenly. Then decorate the bowls with the raw vegetables in parts until they are filled. It looks particularly nice if you don't mix the vegetables, but put them in different parts of the bowl. The vegetables in the bowl absorb a lot of broth and also release a lot of their own juice, which is why the end product tastes less intense than the broth from the stove. Now quickly bring the broth to a hot boil again and pass it through a sieve. Distribute the sieved broth evenly into the bowls until they are full to the brim. Then put the bean sprouts on the vegetables and put the meat on top.

# HARD – 90+ MINUTES

# TRADITIONAL RAMEN SOUP

## INGREDIENTS FOR 4 PORTIONS

- 500g of pork loin or pork loin
- 100ml of soy sauce
- 500g of ramen noodles
- 4 cloves of garlic
- 3 spring onions
- 4 carrots
- 100g of bean sprouts
- 4 eggs
- 1 pinch pepper
- 1 pinch of salt
- 1 tbsp of sugar
- 4 shiitake mushroom or mushrooms
- 1 tbsp of chili flakes (your choice)
- 600ml of vegetable stock

# PREPARATION

Total time: approx. 1 hour 45 minutes

1. Place the pressure cooker on the stove, add a dash of oil and sear the meat on all sides so that it gets to color. Then deglaze with the broth and add the soy sauce. Let everything cook for at least an hour with the lid closed.

2. In the meantime, you can cook the eggs hard and cut the vegetables into slices. Cut the onion into eighths. Add the sugar and the spices to the vegetables so that everything can go straight into the pot.

3. When the meat is cooked, you can take it out and put the pasta with the vegetables in the pot. Then carefully pull the meat apart with two forks so that there are small threads. When you're done, put the meat back in the pot. Stir again and serve.

# VEGAN RAMEN SOUP

## INGREDIENTS FOR 4 PORTIONS

- 250g of mie noodles, vegan
- 1 onion
- 5 garlic cloves
- ½ bundle of spring onions
- 14g shiitake mushroom (dried)
- 1,400ml of vegetable stock
- 2 tbsp of soy sauce
- 1 tbsp of miso paste (light)
- 1 teaspoon of ginger powder
- 2 tbsp of sesame oil for frying

For the vegetables:

- 6 carrots
- 2 pak choi
- 2 tbsp of miso paste (dark)
- 2 tbsp of maple syrup

- 2 tbsp of rice wine vinegar
- 1 tbsp of soy sauce
- 2 tbsp of vegetable oil

Moreover:

- 200g smoked
- 1 tbsp of food starch
- 1 shot of soy sauce
- 1 tbsp of sesame oil

# PREPARATION

Total time: approx. 1 hour 50 minutes

1. Cut half of the onion and slice it roughly into strips, finely chop the garlic. Slice the spring onions and set the green part aside.
2. Heat the sesame oil in a large saucepan and fry the onions for 6 minutes. Add the white part of the spring onions, the garlic, and the ground ginger, and sauté for 2 minutes. Deglaze the onions with 200ml broth and loosen the roast on the bottom of the pot with a wooden spoon. Add the remaining broth, the soy sauce, and the dried mushrooms, and stir in. Bring the soup to a boil once, and then simmer on low heat with the lid closed for 1-2 hours. The longer the soup simmers, the more intense the taste becomes. Season the broth with soy sauce and add the miso paste. Finally, add the Mie noodles to the soup and let them cook in the soup until they have reached the desired bite resistance.
3. Preheat the oven to 220°C. Halve the Pak choi, cut the carrots into bite-size pieces. Mix the remaining ingredients into a sauce. Spread the sauce on the cut surface of the Pak Choi. Swirl the carrot pieces in the remaining sauce and place it on the baking sheet. Cook the carrots in the oven for 30-40 minutes. In the last 10 minutes, place the Pak choi on the tray with the cut surface facing up, and bake with it.
4. Dice the tofu and mix it with 1 tbsp. of starch. Heat the vegetable oil in a pan and fry the tofu all over for 10 minutes with sufficient oil until crispy. Finally, deglaze with a dash of soy sauce.
5. Spread the soup on bowls. Spread the tofu, Pak choi, and carrots over the pasta and garnish everything with the green part of the spring onions.

# SPICY VEGETARIAN RAMEN

## INGREDIENTS FOR 2 PORTIONS

- 180g of ramen noodles
- 2 cups of water
- 1 sheet of algae (kelp, large, or 5 - 10 strips)
- 1 handful of shiitake mushroom or other mushrooms, dried
- 2 tbsp of sesame oil
- 1 onion
- 2 cloves of garlic
- 2cm of ginger
- 1 tbsp of tomato paste
- 1 tbsp of sesame
- 2 tbsp of sake
- 3 tbsp of soy sauce
- 1 tbsp of mirin
- 2 cup of soy milk (soy drink, unsweetened)
- 1 pinch of pepper (white)

- ¼ tbsp of sea salt (ground)
- Chili powder or shichimi togarashi (chili spice mixture)
- 3 eggs
- Corn
- Cabbage
- Soy sauce
- Chili powder
- Some bean sprouts

# PREPARATION

Total time: approx. 2 hours

1. Soak the mushrooms and seaweed in 2 cups of lukewarm water for 30 minutes.
2. In the meantime, you can dice the onion, dice the ginger and press the garlic.
3. Brown the sesame seeds in a hot dry pan and then grind them with a mortar. Then sauté this together with onion, ginger, and garlic in sesame oil, and color it red with tomato paste.
4. Bring the mushroom and seaweed broth to a boil and then remove the mushrooms and seaweed so that only the broth is left. Then set the broth aside.
5. Add the sake, soy sauce, and mirin to the onions, bring to a boil and then pour in soy milk and broth as needed. You have to vary something with the soy milk and the broth, depending on the amount you may have to add a little bit of both. Season with white pepper, salt, and chili spice and, if necessary, season with sake, soy sauce and mirin.
6. Also, prepare the toppings, hard boil, and peel, and then halve the eggs. Season the cabbage with chili powder and soy sauce and cook. Boil the corn and prepare other vegetables if necessary.
7. Finally, cook the noodles according to the package instructions, the best way to use ramen noodles here. Spaghetti is often used as an alternative, but I cannot imagine the taste.
8. When everything is ready, put the noodles in the bowls, distribute the hot broth and fill with toppings.

# RAMEN WITH CHICKEN

## INGREDIENTS FOR 6 PORTIONS

- 1 kg of chicken, a whole or chicken leg
- 2 cloves of garlic
- 1 piece of ginger (approx. 2 cm, peeled)
- 2 spring onion (cleaned)
- Sesame oil
- ½ bar of leek (cleaned)
- 3 carrots (peeled)
- Parsley
- 1 bay leaf
- Salt
- Some peppercorns
- Chili flakes
- Sriracha sauce
- Soy sauce
- 400g of noodles
- Some shiitake mushroom (optional)
- 6 eggs

# PREPARATION

Total time: approx. 1 hour 50 minutes

1. Put the chicken in a saucepan with 1 spring onion, carrots, leek, parsley, bay leaf, peppercorns, salt, and chili flakes (to taste). Cover with water, bring to a boil and simmer in about 1 hour.

2. In the meantime, chop the white side of the second spring onion, the ginger, and the garlic as finely as possible and sauté in sesame oil on medium heat. Finely chopped mushrooms or similar can also be added.

3. Cut the green of the spring onion into rings.

4. If the spices in the sesame oil are well browned, deglaze with a generous portion of soy sauce and sriracha (as desired). Reduce the heat and let the soy sauce caramelize.

5. Remove the chicken from the saucepan and break it open slightly to allow it to evaporate faster. Pour the broth through a sieve and put it back into the pot without the vegetables.

6. Boil water in a small saucepan and add the eggs. Cook to taste for 8-10 minutes and chill well. Peel and cut in half.

7. Pour some of the broth into the pan with the spices, stir well to scrape everything off the floor and season the broth with the resulting seasoning mixture. Remove the meat from the chicken. Cook the pasta in the broth and arrange everything together. Serve sprinkled with the green of the spring onion.

# CHASHU-MEN RAMEN

## INGREDIENTS FOR 4 PORTIONS

- 1 boiling fowl
- 12cm of ginger
- 250ml of soy sauce (japanese)
- 500g of noodles
- 6 toes of garlic
- 1 onion
- 1 bar of leek
- 6 carrots
- 1 nori
- 100g of bean sprouts, fresh
- 4 eggs
- 6 spring onions
- 450g of pork belly or shoulder
- 2 tbsp of mirin (japanese cooking wine)
- 50ml of sake (japanese rice wine)
- 1 tbsp of honey
- 1 tbsp of maple syrup

# PREPARATION

Total time: approx. 1 hours 15 minutes + 3-4 hour for the broth

1. The recipe consists of two broths. You will come to the second one later; first, go to the chicken broth: Add the following ingredients to a large saucepan: the soup chicken, 3 spring onions stick, leek, a peeled onion, 4 peeled cloves of garlic, 4 carrots, a nori leaf, 4 cm peeled ginger. Now that all the ingredients are in the pot, fill in enough water to cover the chicken, add salt, pepper and sugar and heat everything. The broth has to simmer on medium heat for 3-4 hours. If foam forms, skim it off so that the broth later becomes nice and clear.
   When the cooking time is over, sieve the broth and set it aside. The contents of the sieve can be discarded.

2. Now let's take a look at the meat and the second broth:
   First, we peel the remaining two cloves of garlic and the remaining ginger and put both aside. Then we grab a saucepan, add oil and fry the meat on all sides over medium heat. Once this is done, we take out the meat, clean the pot and put it back on the stove at the same heat.

3. Add the following ingredients to the pot: Soy sauce, Mirin, Sake, Peppercorns, Maple syrup, Honey. Stir everything well and bring to a boil. Put the fried meat and the remaining ingredients: the peeled ginger, 2 spring onions and the cloves of garlic in the pot and fill it with enough boiling water until the meat is lightly covered. Now put the lid on the pot and let everything simmer on moderate heat for one to one and a half hours. Turn the meat every now and then. In the meantime, you can cook the eggs hard. As soon as the meat is ready, we take it out of the pot, cut it into slices and sieve this broth.

4. Now that we have both broths ready, you can pour them both together and bring them to a boil again so that the broth. At this point, it is also advisable to season everything and, if necessary, season with soy sauce and/or rice wine. Now boil and drain the noodles, rinse the bean sprouts, and cut a few raw carrots into thin strips. Put some of the vegetable strips, the bean sprouts and the pasta in a bowl, fill up with the hot broth and with a few slices of meat, half an egg and one Garnish with a few spring onion rings.

# JAPANESE NOODLES SOUP WITH CHICKEN BROTH

## INGREDIENTS FOR 4 PORTIONS

- 1 pork loin (pork fillet), in one piece, approximately (approx.) 500g
- 1 soup chicken (frozen)
- 1 piece of ginger root, approx. 8 cm
- Water
- 100ml soy sauce, japanese
- 100ml rice wine or sake
- 500g of soup noodles
- 4 cloves of garlic
- 1 bar of leek
- 4 carrots
- 1 nori sheets
- 100g of bean sprouts (fresh)
- 3 eggs
- 3 spring onions
- Salt and pepper
- 1 tablespoon of sugar

# PREPARATION

Total time: approx. 1 hours 45 minutes + 3-4 hours for the broth

The broth:

1. Mix the soup chicken with a stick of leek, an onion, three to four cloves of garlic, five centimeters of ginger, a pinch of salt, three to four carrots and a handful of algae (optional) in cold water. Add enough water to cover the chicken completely. (Choose pot size so that everything plus two to three liters of water fits in well - a five-liter pot is ideal).

2. Bring to a slow simmer, and let it simmer for at least 3-4 hours. The broth becomes even more delicious with cooking times of 6 - 8 hours. If there is foam, you can skim it off, but it's unnecessary.

3. The broth should not boil too much - just simmer gently. The longer this broth cooks the better. Then sieve the broth. I do not use boiled parts. It is better to use a good real soup chicken, not a chicken.

The loin:

1. Briefly sear the pork loin in a pan on all sides until it is slightly brown. Don't fry too long - just lightly brown. Then put in a saucepan and pour in 100ml soy sauce (I use Kikkoman because it is naturally brewed) and 50ml to 100ml rice wine (I use Chinese rice wine). Add 1 tablespoon of sugar, a sliced spring onion (with the green and only a little of the onion) and 3cm of grated fresh ginger. Pour in a little water so that the loin is almost completely covered with liquid. Then bring the liquid to a simmer. Let it simmer again slightly.

2. After 40 minutes, take the loin out of the liquid and set aside. Then cut the loin into slices (approx. 2 - 3 mm thick) before it comes into the soup.

3. The loin should come from a good butcher - there are amazing quality differences. A good loin is very tender and juicy after this procedure, not tough and dry.

The eggs:

1.  Cook four eggs hard and peel them. Put the eggs in the loin broth and simmer for 10 minutes. Turn again and again so that they are evenly browned by the brew. When they're done, cut them in half and set them aside.

The pasta:

1.  You can make your own noodles while the broths are cooking (recipes for this can be found in this book) or use Chinese soup noodles from the Asian shop. I've had very good experiences with quick noodles, and even spaghetti in them tastes very good. If you have a well-stocked Asian shop, you may even get ramen noodles or fresh ramen noodles.

2.  According to the instructions, always cook the pasta strictly hard, not too soft.

The soup:

1.  When the chicken broth is ready, put it in a saucepan with the loin broth and season with a few tablespoons of soy sauce and another shot of rice wine. You can add salt, but the soy sauce should actually provide enough salt. Then let everything boil again. You can also add water, depending on how strong or diluted you want the soup. I leave the broth pure without adding water. When the soup cooks, all other ingredients should be ready for the next step, especially the pasta.

Garnish:

1.  Scald the bean sprouts with hot water in a sieve. Cut the green of two spring onions into rings. Cut small strips (approx. 2 x 3 cm) from the nori sheets.

The finish:

1.  Put the soup in a bowl and add enough pasta, so that the pasta reaches just below the surface.

2. Add two or three slices of the loin. The loin can be sprinkled with coarse pepper.

3. Place half an egg on the edge of the shell with the egg yolk facing up.

4. Sprinkle a small handful of sprouts and spring onions over it and then add the nori leaf.

5. Enjoy the sight of the soup. Eating with chopsticks and sipping the broth loudly - it tastes best this way.

Note:

- The cooked loin can also be placed on a bowl of rice and poured over with the loin broth. Also very tasty as an alternative dish.

The soup is actually not complex, but it takes a lot of time because all the ingredients have to be cooked for a long time to develop a unique taste. It really pays off not to get hectic with the broth, and allow it the necessary cooking time. The recipe is a kind of basic recipe. The broth can be further refined (e.g. with algae or dashi) or pork bones can also be cooked alongside the chicken. A whole lot is also suitable as an inlay for the soup - just experiment or check out what others are doing online.
The soup is very invigorating and also amazingly filling.

# NOODLES SOUP WITH CHICKEN

## INGREDIENTS FOR 6 PORTIONS

For the broth:

- 1 boiling fowl
- 4 carrots
- 1 leek
- 4 cloves of garlic
- 3cm of ginger root
- 1 pinch of salt

For the brew:

- 100ml of soy sauce
- 80ml of sake or chinese wine, in need gin or vodka
- 2 spring onions
- 3cm of ginger root

Moreover:

- 4 eggs
- 500g of ramen noodles (spaghetti broken through 3 times is sufficient in an emergency)
- Pepper
- Some spring onion (cut into rings, for decoration)

# PREPARATION

Total time: approx. 1 hours 30 minutes + 3-4 hours for the broth

The broth:

1. Gently boil the soup chicken, carrots, leeks, cloves of garlic, and ginger in salted water for 3 - 4 hours.
2. Lift the chicken out of the broth and let it cool slightly. Detach the meat from the bones and cut it into edible pieces.
3. Boil and peel the eggs hard.

For the brew:

1. Heat in a saucepan with a lid of soy sauce, sake or similar. Cut 2 spring onions into small rings and add small ginger. Fold in the meat, and then simmer everything on a low flame for about 10 minutes with the lid closed. Insert the eggs and turn more often in the brew. Let everything simmer for another 10 minutes.
2. Cook the pasta bite-proof and pour off according to the instructions.
3. Remove the leek and garlic from the broth and discard. Cut the carrots into slices and set them aside. Pour the broth through a sieve into another large saucepan to get a nice clear broth. Pepper the broth.
4. Lift the meat and eggs out of the broth. Stir the broth from soy sauce into the broth.
5. Provide bowls. Pour in the broth, add the noodles, insert 2 halves of a cut egg, put on the meat and decorate with spring onion rings. Add the carrot slices. If necessary, soy sauce can also be added.

# NOODLES SOUP WITH CHICKEN THIGH

## INGREDIENTS FOR 4 PORTIONS

- 400g of wheat flour
- 180ml of mineral water (cold)
- 5g of salt
- 4 chicken legs
- 1 spring onion
- 1 carrot
- 1 small chinese cabbage
- 100g of bean sprouts
- 500ml of water
- 15g dashi no moto (dashi stock base made of bonito fish powder)
- 3 tbsp of soy sauce
- 3 tbsp of mirin
- 1 tbsp of sugar
- 2 tbsp of oil (tasteless)

# PREPARATION

Total time approx. 1 hour 45 minutes

1. For the Udon noodles, mix the flour with the salt and the cold mineral water until a firm dough is formed. Ideally, it is done with a kneading machine for 5 minutes or until the thickness of the pasta is reached. They have to be firm; otherwise, they will fall apart in the hot water. Let the dough cool for 30 minutes.

2. In the meantime, bone the chicken drumsticks and leave them on the skin. Cut the soft cabbage portion from the top of the Chinese cabbage and the hard stalk below. Cut the middle part into bite-size pieces. Wash the bean sprouts, remove dry leaves and roots from the spring onions, wash and cut into thin diagonal slices. Peel the carrots and cut them into thin strips, preferably with an asparagus peeler. Again, it should be cut into bite-size pieces. Roll out the Udon dough and cut into strips of approx. 5mm thick pasta in a pasta machine. If you do not have a pasta machine, you have to fold the dough three to four times (dust well with flour so that it does not stick) and then cut into 5mm strips with the largest knife.

3. Heat soy sauce, mirin, water, dashi no moto, sugar, and half of the oil in a saucepan. Add the carrot and Chinese cabbage and simmer for about 5 minutes. Let the other half of the oil heat up in a pan and fry the chicken legs with the skin side down for about 5 minutes (or until the skin is brown), then turn and fry.

4. Pour the pasta water as usual and put the Udon noodles in deep plates and place the soybean sprouts and the spring onion rings on them, put the hot soup on the noodles and top the whole thing with the fried chicken drumstick, from the pan onto a piece of kitchen paper (to absorb the excess fat) and then cut into bite-size pieces with a sharp butcher knife.

# VEGETABLE AND MUSHROOM PAN

## INGREDIENTS FOR 4 PORTIONS

For the marinade:

- 3 tbsp of soy sauce
- 1 tbsp of honey
- 1 tbsp of sesame oil
- 1 clove of garlic
- 1 small piece of ginger root
- Chili
- Lemon pepper

Moreover:

- 200g of beefsteak
- 250g of udon noodles
- 40g of shiitake mushroom, dried
- 250g of mushrooms, brown
- 1 bunch spring onions

- 200g of sugar snap
- 250g of paprika
- 6 tbsp of soy sauce
- 1 tbsp of oil
- 1 tbsp of sesame

# PREPARATION

Total time approx. 3 hours 40 minutes

1. Mix the ingredients for the marinade. Cut the steak into fine strips and let it marinate for 2-3 hours.

2. Let the shiitake mushrooms soak for 1 hour according to the package instructions.

3. In the meantime, wash and prepare the vegetables. Clean the mushrooms and cut them into slices or cubes. Cut the spring onions into rings. Cut the bell pepper into cubes. Blanch the sugar snap peas briefly in boiling water. If fresh ones are used, first pull off the fine threads on the side with a sharp knife.

4. Cook the Udon noodles according to the package instructions (approx. 13 minutes) and drain well.

5. Sear the meat for 1 minute and remove from the pan. Then sear the peppers until firm and add the mushrooms. When the mushrooms are well browned, add sugar snap peas, spring onions, and pasta and stir everything well.

6. Add the meat again. Add 6 tablespoons of soy sauce and stir well again.

7. Finally, sprinkle 1-2 tablespoons of sesame over the food, depending on your taste.

# RICE NOODLES AND CHICKEN

## INGREDIENTS FOR 2 PORTIONS

- 150g of rice noodles (japanese)
- 2m in size of chicken breasts
- 1 tbsp of rapeseed oil or sesame oil
- 1 carrot
- 1 bar of leek
- 8 mushrooms (fresh)
- 150g spring onions
- Chili pepper (fresh)
- ½ glass of bamboo shoot
- 2 toes of garlic
- 1 piece of ginger (approx. 1 cm x 1 cm x 1 cm)
- 1 chili pepper (red, dried)
- 4 tbsp of soy sauce light)
- 2 tbsp of fish sauce
- 50 ml of chicken broth
- 1 tbsp of coriander seeds
- 1 tbsp of sesame (lien ying goma), toasted
- Black pepper

# PREPARATION

Total time: approx. 1 hour 45 minutes

1. Cut the chicken breasts into strips approx. 1cm thick with 3 tablespoons of light soy sauce (Please be very careful with this, chicken breasts are often of different sizes. Make sure that the meat "looks marinated"), a clove of garlic and mix with a teaspoon of toasted sesame seeds, and then put in a bowl.

2. Letting it simmer for an hour should be the most pragmatic case, but for everyday life, it is enough to keep the meat in the sauce while slicing vegetables.

3. Then heat the rapeseed or sesame oil in a wok or wok pan. With sesame oil, I advise extreme caution when dosing, since it is very aromatic. Sauté finely chopped garlic, also finely chopped ginger as well as the dried chili and coriander seeds before frying the meat together with the soy sauce for approx. 2-3 minutes. I personally just break open the pod and put the seeds in the oil. It would also be conceivable to place the pod completely in the oil and remove it before adding the meat. In this way, the oil is pleasantly flavored and the sharpness is limited.

4. Take the meat out again and set it aside. Add the leek rings, carrot slices, the mushrooms, and the chili peppers (I take it very mildly, peppers are an excellent alternative) in the remaining oil and steam for a few minutes. Then deglaze with a dash of soy sauce and 2 tablespoons of fish sauce. Then mix in the bamboo saplings and spring onions, let them warm briefly and add the meat again.

5. With the vegetables, the soy and fish sauce, the dish should already have developed enough liquid. To curb and round off the taste, I recommend a little chicken broth. I would avoid salt for this dish because the soy sauce is already very salty.

6. Shortly before serving, mix in the rice noodles that were previously prepared according to the package description. Sprinkle some sesame seeds on the plate.

7. Tip: If you have no experience with fish sauce, please dose it a little more sparingly and do not let the smell deter you. This flies in the pot after a few seconds.

# SUKIYAKI

## INGREDIENTS FOR 4 PORTIONS

- 250g of tofu
- 150g of glass noodles (japanese)
- 10 shiitake mushrooms
- 100g of mushrooms (enoki mushrooms) or oyster mushrooms
- 200g of herbs (shungiku or salads chrysanthemum) or spinach leaves
- 2 bars of leek
- 400g of chinese cabbage
- 600g of entrecote (cut into 2mm thin slices)
- 3 tbsp of vegetable oil
- 120ml of soy sauce (japanese)
- 120ml of mirin
- 4 eggs (fresh)
- 2 tbsp of sugar

# PREPARATION

Total time: approx. 2 hours 20 minutes

1. Put the tofu briefly in cold water, drain and pat dry carefully. Cut into 16 pieces. Boil the noodles in plenty of water for about 5 minutes and drain. For dried shiitake mushrooms, pour boiling water over them and let them soak in the water for 20 minutes. Remove the stems as they can be very hard. Wipe the mushrooms with a cloth, leave part of it whole and cut part into triangles. Wash the Enoki and remove the brown section. Clean and wash the Shungiku.

2. Clean and wash the Chinese cabbage and cut the leaves into pieces about 10cm long. Bring water to a boil in a saucepan. Blanch the cabbage for about 5 minutes, drain and press a little so that it is not too watery. Remove the leek from roots and green leaves and wash. Cut diagonally into pieces about 5cm long. It is best to cut the entrecote thinly if it has been briefly frozen. Decorate the ingredients including entrecote on a large platter. Add chopsticks or forks.

3. For the sauces, bring the soy sauce, mirin, and sugar to a short boil in a saucepan. Remove 150ml and put it in a jug. Add 50ml of water to the remaining sauce and put the diluted sauce in a second jug.

4. Place a fresh, raw egg in each bowl and whisk. Place a hotplate or gas burner with a Sukiyaki pot, available in an Asian shop, or a roasting pan on the table and heat. Add oil and briefly fry several slices of meat. Add about half of the undiluted sauce. Add some of the vegetables and some tofu. When the sauce is boiling, add a portion of the glass noodles and cook with tofu, meat, and vegetables for 6-8 minutes.

5. Each person at the table serves himself with chopsticks or forks from the Sukiyaki pot. The meat and other ingredients are briefly dipped in the egg before they are eaten.

6. You determine the rhythm in which to eat and put meat, vegetables and other ingredients in the pot. Even while it is cooking, you can use the pot and add new ingredients. Do not put too many ingredients in the pot at once. Top up the sauce again and again during preparation. First, use undiluted and then the diluted sauce so that the taste does not become too intense. (Approx. 700 Kcal per serving).

# SZECHUAN PEPPER CHICKEN

## INGREDIENTS FOR 4 PORTIONS

- 3 tbsp of szechuan pepper
- 2 cloves of garlic
- 1 tbsp of ginger (chopped)
- 3 tbsp of food starch
- 2 tbsp of soy sauce (dark)
- 600g of chicken thighs
- 100g of ramen noodles
- 3 tbsp of vegetable oil
- 1 onion
- 1 pepper (yellow)
- 1 bell pepper (red)
- 100g of sweet peas
- 80ml of chicken broth

# PREPARATION

Total time: approx. 2 hours 40 minutes

1.  Roast the Szechuan pepper without oil until it starts to smell. Then mortar and mix with the chopped cloves of garlic, ginger, soy sauce, and cornstarch.

2.  Skin the chicken legs, remove the meat from the bones and cut into strips. Mix well with the previously made marinade and leave covered for two hours in the fridge.

3.  Thinly strip the two peppers, cut the onion into rings. Cook the pasta in boiling salted water and drain.

4.  Fry the chicken in portions in hot vegetable oil. Remove from the wok or pan and cook the peppers, the onion rings, and the peas in the roast stock for two to three minutes, stirring constantly. If canned peas are used, then let the temperature rise briefly at the end. Add the chicken broth and bring to a boil. The sauce thickens due to the starch in the marinade. Add the chicken strips and the pasta to the hot mixture and mix. It can then be served immediately.

Made in the USA
Coppell, TX
08 December 2020

43363523R20197